IMAGES
of America

PRESERVING
BALLARD

1920

This photograph of a young woman was part of the Peterson Collection donated to the Ballard Historical Society. She is looking down through a Kodak Brownie box camera, the first amateur and affordable camera, introduced in 1900 to the American market. Many of the Peterson Collection images, spanning 1910 to 1930, appear in this book. (Courtesy of the Peterson Collection, Ballard Historical Society.)

ON THE COVER: In the 1910s and 1920s, progressive women shifted away from long skirts and dresses to bloomers, such as these young women are wearing while taking a coastal stroll on the railroad tracks. Bloomers were associated with the campaign for women's voting rights. The state of Washington had a strong and active suffrage movement since its early pioneer days. In 1910, Washington was the fifth state to give women the right to vote, a full decade before women were given the right to vote nationally through the 14th Amendment to the US Constitution in 1920. (Courtesy of the Peterson Collection, Ballard Historical Society.)

IMAGES
of America

PRESERVING
BALLARD

Ballard Historical Society

ARCADIA
PUBLISHING

Published by Arcadia Publishing
Charleston, South Carolina

Library of Congress Control Number: 2021952819

For all general information, please contact Arcadia Publishing:
Telephone 843-853-2070
Fax 843-853-0044
E-mail sales@arcadiapublishing.com
For customer service and orders:
Toll-Free 1-888-313-2665

Visit us on the Internet at www.arcadiapublishing.com

*To the many Ballard residents who have cared for and
contributed to Ballard over the decades and in memory of
Rob Mattson, Ballard's unofficial mayor, who was Ballard
Neighborhood District coordinator during his long career.*

CONTENTS

ACKNOWLEDGMENTS

Ballard Historical Society acknowledges that Ballard lies on the unceded traditional land of the first people of Seattle, the Duwamish. We honor their past and present heritage with gratitude.

A thank-you is owed to the trustees of the Ballard Historical Society, Lesli Cook, Laura K. Cooper, Davidya Kasperzyk, Cass O'Callaghan, Zachary Nesgoda, Kris Royer Collins, and Mary Schile, for their work compiling this book. Special thanks go to the *Preserving Ballard* workgroup, Laura Cooper, Alison DeRiemer of National Nordic Museum, Abby Inpanbutr of Art and Soul Photo Inc., and Peggy Sturdivant, At Large in Ballard. Additional thanks are given to Jay Craig, Ballard's bell-keeper; Tod Gangler, photographer; Larry Johnson, architect; John LaMont, Special Collections at the Seattle Public Library; Stephen Lundgren, local historian; Matt Stevenson of CORE GIS; and the dozens of volunteers who contributed to Mapping Historic Ballard. Additionally, thanks go to the many individuals preceding Ballard Historical Society's current board and members who contributed by aggregating our collection and making this work possible.

We would also like to thank the following publications and associated organizations for information and support: the *Ballard News Tribune* for decades of coverage, Paul Dorpat's Then and Now column, *Passport to Ballard*, *Voices of Ballard*, *Native Seattle*, Museum of History and Industry (MOHAI) Photographic Archives, Puget Sound Regional Archives, and the University of Washington Special Collections for preserving images and writings on Ballard. We also thank King County's 4Culture and the City of Seattle for funding several of our projects.

Unless otherwise noted, all images contained in this book are from the Ballard Historical Society Archives.

INTRODUCTION

Ballard is located in the northwest corner of Seattle along Salmon Bay and Puget Sound, now also called the Salish Sea. Ballard's identity and strong sense of place is distinctly separate from the rest of Seattle. This legacy springs from its origins as the independent City of Ballard, established 1889.

Historically, the Salmon Bay area was home to the Shilshole branch of the Duwamish People. The interior was heavily forested with cedar and fir. Ira Utter and Osbourne Hall filed a homestead claim for the land that is now Ballard in 1852—the same year the Arthur Denny Party landed in Seattle. Hall sold out to Utter, who continued to live alone on his 820 acres on Salmon Bay for almost 20 years.

Ballard's first wave of development occurred in 1871 when D.W. Crooks bought 720 acres from Ira Utter. In 1882, it was platted into 10-acre plots with 60-foot-wide streets and called Farmdale. In 1887, three main investors, Capt. William Ballard (for whom Ballard was named), Thomas Burke, and John Leary formed the West Coast Improvement Company to profit from their combined land holdings. Gilman Park, with 3,000 residential lots measuring 50 feet by 100 feet and large lots on the waterfront for industrial use, followed in 1889. The profit-seeking company then lured businesses and promoted infrastructure to make Ballard an attractive place to live.

The City of Ballard was Washington's first incorporated community after statehood in 1890. Ballard prospered primarily because of the lumber and shingle mills along the industrial waterfront and, later, its maritime industry. Only a block from the mills, a bustling commercial district developed along Ballard Avenue. In the early 1900s, masonry structures in keeping with prosperity and civic pride quickly replaced wooden storefronts. Ballard City Hall at the north end of Ballard Avenue housed Ballard's city council and jail. In 1904, Ballard built the greater Seattle area's first Carnegie library (still standing, now privately owned). Ballard had its own hospital and fire department. Ballard also had many bars and, according to urban myth, an equal number of churches! Several church buildings still stand along Twentieth Avenue NW.

Like other communities on the outskirts of Seattle, Ballard quickly outgrew its resources. Seattle's water source was the Cedar River; Ballard had no access to it. Motivated to ensure access to water for its 15,000 citizens, residents voted for annexation to Seattle in 1907. Although Ballard's city hall was draped in black that day, Ballard did not lose its identity after annexation. Ballard continued to prosper. The fishing and boatbuilding industries, primarily started as small family businesses, were growing in importance. In 1914, Fishermen's Terminal was established on the south shore of Shilshole Bay. Its facilities still accommodate one of the largest fishing fleets on the West Coast. In 1916, the Ballard Locks and the Ship Canal project forever separated the freshwater shoreline from the saltwater tide and vastly improved the area for industry. This industry provided livelihoods for generations to follow.

Today, Ballard is known for many things: its strong Scandinavian ties, its renowned fishing fleet and maritime industry, the Ballard Locks, the National Nordic Museum, the Ballard Farmer's Market, and, most importantly, a strong independent identity and spirit. A thriving business district remains largely intact as the Ballard Avenue portion was protected by Seattle City Ordinance as a Historic Landmark District in 1976. Visitors and residents can enjoy a stroll past buildings listed in the National Register of Historic Places.

Ballard has certainly grown in population. Yet, some families still can trace their roots to Ballard pioneers. These families and others have contributed to rich archives of photography collections and oral histories, which are housed at institutions such as the National Nordic Museum, Ballard High School Foundation, and Ballard Historical Society. Partnerships between businesses, schools, and citizens such as the Centennial Committee and Ballard Historical Society were made possible by Ballard's infrastructure and culture. Recent preservation efforts include "Bring the Ring Back to Ballard," Mapping Historic Ballard, and Heritage Preservation.

This photograph collection depicting Ballard is representative of certain major periods in Ballard's history, but it is by no means inclusive. There are few records of the land or peoples before it was homesteaded. However, the pace of development occurred rapidly during its boom periods. While Ballard boomed, first as a "Shingle Capital," so did its nightlife, from dance halls to taverns. As pioneers and immigrants prospered, the first homes became larger, and fishermen's shacks often became Craftsman-style homes up on the hill. In the postwar period of the 1940s and 1950s, the original plats were divided, making for a checkerboard of housing styles. Oral histories from the residents of these different times help give voice to the photographs of bygone Ballard days.

One

BEFORE BALLARD

Like much of the Puget Sound region, Ballard is built on a layer of glacial moraine, which was deposited in the last ice age, on top of a layer of sand, on top of a layer of clay. The land slopes south down to Salmon Bay from Eighty-third Street NW and is comprised of several rolls east to west until the high bank drop-off down to the edge of Puget Sound where the beach is relatively narrow.

Ballard is primarily within the North Salmon Bay watershed. Historic streams, now underground in combined culverts, run down Eighth Avenue, Twenty-fourth Avenue, and Twenty-eighth Avenue to Salmon Bay. The land was covered in a primeval forest of trees, some of which were 1,000 years old, with an edge at the shore. The shore at Salmon Bay provided plentiful seafood, including salmon, which congregated there before heading upstream, for the Shilshole branch of the Duwamish People. Oral tradition speaks of longhouses on the coast near Salmon Bay. Canoes were the main form of transportation for both the Native Americans and the first settlers as the forests were too dense to move through easily. Several site-specific names for the Ballard area have been translated into English, including one for the mouth of Salmon Bay; its name roughly translates to "threading a bead," which refers to the shape of Salmon Bay before moving farther up the narrowing waterway toward what is now Fremont.

There is little information and less pictorial documentation about Ballard before settlement. There were already relatively few Native Americans living in the Ballard area when Ira Utter arrived as the first documented non-native settler in the early 1850s. Early accounts of the Puget Sound region indicate that waves of disease, either brought by non-native traders or, perhaps, that traveled along precontact trade routes, eradicated many native peoples. Additionally, oral tradition tells of repeated plundering raids from the North and the peoples of this region melting into the woods to try to avoid capture. By the 1850s, the Ballard area was down to a few dozen Indigenous people.

Ira Sutter had a good relationship with the Shilshole peoples and, for almost two decades, was the only non-native settler on Salmon Bay. After he died and his holdings were sold off, more settlers moved in. By this time, it was common policy to relocate Native Americans off desirable land, so the remaining Shilshole peoples were moved to combined tribal reservations. A few stayed, married non-native settlers, and raised families in the area. Like Princess Angeline (Kikisoblu), Chief Seattle's daughter in Seattle, Salmon Bay Charlie (Hwehlchtid) and his wife, Madeline (Chilohleetsa), well known in the Ballard area, refused to leave and continued to live on Salmon Bay until around 1914, when Madeline passed away.

Puget Sound, or Salish Sea, is a system of interconnected marine waterways and basins connected to the Strait of Juan de Fuca and the Pacific Ocean. With an average depth of 205 feet and maximum depth of 930 feet, Puget Sound has Ballard nestled on its eastern shore at latitude 47 40' 33" N and longitude 122 23' 14" W. The saltwater of Puget Sound and the freshwater of Salmon Bay flank the community. These photographs were taken before the construction of the Hiram M. Chittenden Locks provided a navigable connection between the two. The photograph above looks east; the photograph below looks west.

This house belonged to Salmon Bay Charlie (Hwehlchtid) and his wife, Madeline (Chilohleetsa). Before the settling of Seattle, the land surrounding Salmon Bay was inhabited by the Shilshole branch of the Duwamish People, who thrived from the plentiful salmon and shellfish. The name Shilshole (šilšul) in the Puget Sound Salish Indian language sometimes translates to "tuck away a little bit." Although Ballard has changed greatly, it still feels tucked away a bit from the hubbub of Seattle. The fresh air coming off the Puget Sound gives Ballard its temperate maritime climate. Anders Wilse took this c. 1897 photograph. (Courtesy of the National Nordic Museum.)

A *Salish Welcome* (2010) by renowned Native American artist Marvin Oliver represents the life cycle of Pacific salmon. It stands above the Salmon Bay Natural Area, the last wooded shoreline in Ballard, near the ship canal and the railroad bridge. The land for this natural area was purchased through the efforts of local nonprofit Groundswell NW. The area protects over 680 feet of undeveloped estuarine shoreline essential as salmon habitat since salmon are anadromous fish and need time to adjust between the saltwaters of Puget Sound and the freshwaters above the locks. (Courtesy of Laura K. Cooper.)

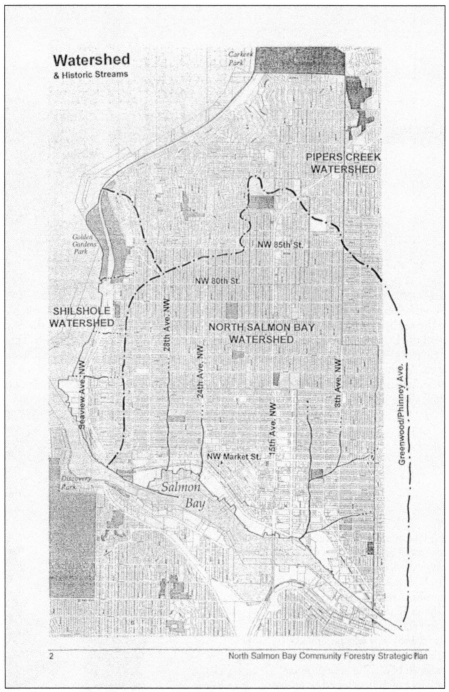

Carkeek
Park

PIPERS CREEK
WATERSHED

Golden
Gardens
Park

NW 85th St.

NW 80th St.

SHILSHOLE
WATERSHED

NORTH SALMON BAY
WATERSHED

28th Ave. NW.

24th Ave. NW

15th Ave. NW

3th Ave. NW

Seaview Ave. NW

Greenwood/Phinney Ave.

NW Market St.

Discovery
Park

*Salmon
Bay*

2   North Salmon Bay Community Forestry Strategic Plan

This map shows Ballard is primarily in the Salmon Bay Watershed. Three streams historically ran south downhill to Salmon Bay. Two other streams ran west and northwest toward Puget Sound. They have all been culverted over time. Ballard pioneer Margaret Wandrey recalled a beautiful salmon-filled stream running past her property near Eleventh Avenue. One of the streams was attributed with supernatural power and referred to as Spirit Canoe Creek by the local Native Americans. (Courtesy of Davidya Kasperzyk.)

Two

BALLARD BOOMS

The city of Ballard prospered primarily because of its lumber and shingle mills along the industrial waterfront. Ballard was the ideal location for timber mills. Captain Ballard convinced Charles Stimson to build Stimson's Mill on Salmon Bay. The Seattle Cedar Company followed in 1890. Ballard's topography slopes down to the water. When its virgin forest was cut, it could be rolled down to the mills, and its boards and shingles were carried away by ship. Later, logs cut from surrounding areas were tied together in large rafts, known as log booms, and transported to Ballard via Salmon Bay. Ballard was able to come to Seattle's rescue after the 1889 citywide fire, which devastated the downtown area. Ballard aided in the rebuilding of the city with lumber. The number of mills climbed with the influx of immigrants. By 1905, more red cedar shingles were being produced in Ballard's shingle mills than in any other community nationwide, earning Ballard the nickname "Shingletown." Ballard was also called the shingle capital of the world. Ballard's economy eventually changed, and the last lumber mill closed in the early 1960s.

In the early 20th century, Ballard's fishing and boatbuilding industries, begun by small family operations, grew in importance. The Ballard Locks, built between 1912 and 1917, and the Ship Canal project, constructed between 1911 and 1934, provided a sheltered harbor and freshwater port for the fishing fleet. In 1914, the Port of Seattle established Fishermen's Terminal on the south shore of Salmon Bay. Its facilities continue to support one of the largest fishing fleets on the West Coast, and its supporting maritime industry has provided livelihoods for generations. Sawmills, boiler works, boatbuilding, manufacturing, foundries, construction, and fishing supplies were all traditional Ballard industries. The Ballard Locks is now second in the world to only the Panama Canal in number of boats that move through it every day and is the third-most popular tourist destination in Seattle, after the Space Needle and Pike Place Market. Marine traffic is recreational as well as commercial.

This photograph depicts boards stacked for air-drying. In 1895, Ballard was informally deemed the "Shingle Mill Capital of the World." With a mere nine mills, Ballard's shingle output exceeded all other major milling centers in the United States. Later, in its heyday, Ballard had 18 shingle mills. The decline of the Salmon Bay mills started during the Great Depression, with a national slowdown in construction. In time, this factor, combined with safety issues, a shift in consumer preference to asphalt shingles, and a decline in availability of cedar, brought about the demise of this Ballard industry.

Stimson Mill was one of Ballard's first mills. Charles D. Stimson was originally in timber in Michigan, but the forest resources there became depleted, so he moved west. This picture shows a massive log destined for Stimson Mill in Ballard. Stimson Mill closed in the 1960s, and the mill site is now holds an office complex, warehouse, and modern marina. (Courtesy of MOHAI.)

Looking up Vernon Avenue from Shilshole Avenue, the Stimson Mill office can be seen on the left side of the photograph with Ballard Avenue in the distance. This distinctive 1912 building, designed by prominent architect Kirtland Cutter, who also designed the Seattle's Rainier Club, is still there today.

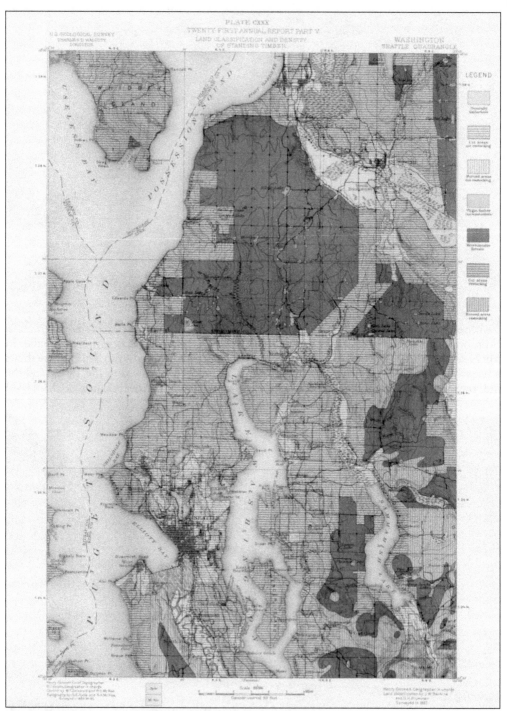

This 1897 US Geological Survey Land Classification and Density of Standing Timber map of the Seattle quadrant shows that Ballard's timber has already been harvested. The earliest mills had ready access to Ballard's forested land, but even before the turn of the century, that stock was gone. Ballard remained a "Shingle Capital," but the focus shifted to maritime means of bringing timber to the mills by using the Government Locks. (Courtesy of Allan MacLeod.)

16

Early Ballard's payroll was closely linked to the timber mills. Many of the smaller houses in Ballard were built as mill workers' homes. Once a "shingletown," Ballard suffered from changing tastes in building materials in the 1920s. The Ballard mills experienced reduced production and long periods of inactivity. Shingle weavers were forced to go on the dole. During the Depression, the demand for cedar shingles stopped almost entirely when the national building industry came to a halt. The Ballard shingle mill industry never recovered.

Log booms, or rafts of logs, were as common a sight in Salmon Bay during the mill years as were the tall conical burners used to dispose of wood debris produced in the milling process. Stifling smoke would scatter a light layer of ash, which came to be known as "Ballard snow." Unfortunately, fires at the mills were fairly common. The caption on the back of the photograph below reads, "May 1958—What was left of the mill after the fire." The Seattle Cedar Mill was one of Ballard's last mills.

These photographs show the Bascule Bridge, completed in 1914. However, this was not Ballard's first railroad bridge. The first railroad bridge, from 1890, was initially used by the Seattle & Montana Railroad Company and, later, by the Great Northern Railroad and other street railways. Its large curved wooden trestle near Fourteenth Avenue NW ran along the north shore of Salmon Bay. With the development of the locks, the railroad bridge was rerouted, and trains started to travel up the coast, as they still do today on the Bascule Bridge.

Naturally shallow, Salmon Bay was formerly a saltwater tidal estuary used as a log harbor where on any given day one could see thousands of logs in its numerous log booms. In 1906, roughly $285,000 was appropriated for dredging and widening Salmon Bay in anticipation of its importance as a harbor on the new ship canal.

In 1916, both recently constructed lock gates were closed, and the level of Salmon Bay rose to the same level as Lake Union and became a freshwater extension of Lakes Union and Washington. The bay had a depth of 12 feet at low tide. Asahel Curtis (1874–1941), photographer and brother of photographer Edward Curtis, took this photograph from Queen Anne, looking north to Ballard; it shows the Fourteenth Avenue bridge with a separate train bridge at about Fifteenth Avenue.

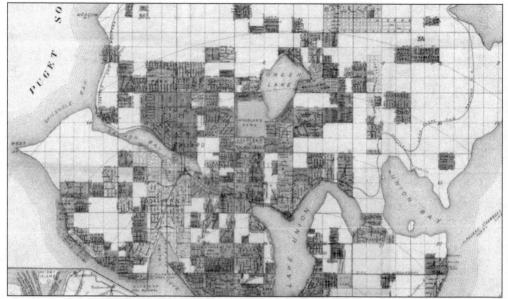

The linked lake system with access to Puget Sound that is now taken for granted was once just an idea. In 1854, Judge Thomas Mercer saw the feasibility of connecting Puget Sound to Lake Washington and named Lake Union for its potential as the link. Harvey Pike dug a ditch between the two bodies of water using a wheelbarrow, pick, and shovel. Pike's primary objective was to increase the value of his own land. The project grew and resulted in the current lake system with access to Puget Sound through the locks. The canal is about eight miles long from Puget Sound to Lake Washington. It also provides a freshwater port for Seattle's fishing fleet. This detail from Anderson's 1890 New Guide Map of the City of Seattle and Environs shows what the area looked like before the ship canal. (Courtesy of Allan MacLeod.)

Taken from the Magnolia slope of Salmon Bay, this 1904 photograph shows Ballard's extensive mill activity and boat works. At the turn of the century, the federal government signed a plan to dredge the canal route from Shilshole Bay to the Salmon Bay wharves in Ballard. This deepening of Salmon Bay allowed logs to be brought directly to the mills on large deep-hulled vessels, and then finished lumber could be loaded onto vessels on their way to deep water in the sound. The recovered dredge materials were used to fill in the tidal back bay wetlands of southeastern Ballard and along the southern edges of the mill district adjacent to the canal, elevating streets up to a height of 16 feet. (Photograph by Asahel Curtis.)

Twenty-five Chinese laborers dug the canal portion at the Ballard Locks. Eventually, it would take a total of 300 men to complete the locks. Not one man died during the construction—a rarity for big engineering projects of the day. The Government Locks used 200,000 cubic yards of cement; some four million cubic yards were used for the entire canal. Much of the dredged sludge and dirt became the topsoil for the Carl S. English Jr. Botanical Gardens on the north side.

The Ballard Locks serve approximately 50,000 boats a year and are second in worldwide usage to the Panama Canal. For vessels going through the locks, it is free and open 24 hours a day because it is run by the US Army Corps of Engineers and funded through the Army's US Presidential budget, a great boon to the local economy. Below is a photograph showing a log boom going through the locks on its way to one of the Ballard mills. (Below, courtesy of MOHAI.)

The Hiram M. Chittenden Locks have been an integral part of Ballard and the waterways around Seattle for over a century. They are still heavily used by working vessels and pleasure craft, like the one depicted above. The locks comprise approximately 17 acres, 7 of which are botanical gardens. The locks were named in honor of Maj. Hiram Martin Chittenden, the engineer who designed and oversaw construction of the locks. The Carl S. English Jr. Botanical Gardens were named after the landscape architect who transformed the mounds of construction dirt left over after the creation of the locks into the English-style botanical gardens. English spent 43 years planting and tending the gardens. Both the locks and the botanical gardens are free to the public. The National Register of Historic Places embraced the locks in 1978. Pictured below, women of the Ballard Historical Society celebrate the 100th anniversary of the Ballard Locks. (Below, courtesy of Mary Schile.)

Immigrants brought shipbuilding and carpentry skills to Ballard, which utilized its citizens' expertise to build boats ranging from tugs and fishing schooners to barges. Along with boatbuilding itself, countless other industries sprang up to support the boatbuilding industry, like dry docks, navigational suppliers, engine distributors, icehouses, ship chandlers, and suppliers of food and fuel. Ballard had plenty of wood for building boats, and many slab burners, like the one shown on the left side of the above photograph. These distinctively shaped structures are frequently seen in old pictures of the Ballard skyline. The burners were used primarily for burning the waste created while turning timber into finished products.

It is highly unlikely that the bottle held by this woman contains champagne. This image of the launch of the SS *Western King* was taken on January 3, 1918, during the "dry years" of Prohibition. Local shipyard J.F. Duthie expanded during World War I to build steel-hulled cargo ships.

On October 26, 1912, the *Forest L. Crosby* was launched in the midst of Ballard's shingle mills at the Cook & Lake yards. It was the 37th towboat built for the Washington Tug & Barge Company. Fishing boats, scows for fish buyers, power scows built for the Army, lifeboats, and tugboats were all built in boatyards along Salmon Bay. Boatbuilding is still an active industry in Ballard.

This photograph celebrates the opening day of Fishermen's Terminal, owned and operated by the Port of Seattle since 1914. Currently, it has the capacity to moor over 700 vessels, and the majority are still fishing boats. Fishing has been one of the most profitable and dangerous industries in Ballard. Ballard's maritime community has fished for a variety of marine life, including herring, cod, albacore, shark, shrimp, pollack, and crab, but over the last century, the most consistent "money fish" have been salmon and halibut. The *Ballard Tribune* stated on July 2, 1936, "The fishing industry wields tremendous influence on Seattle payrolls." Today, Fishermen's Terminal is not only a hub of the fishing industry, but also home to seafood restaurants, fish markets, and some recreational vessels.

The national news of July 4, 1917, focused on the war in Europe. Patriotism reached new heights, and the country's birthday was a perfect time to rally together. However, Ballard's attention was focused on the formal opening of the Government Locks and the Lake Washington Ship Canal. This event drew nearly half of Seattle's 360,000 residents to watch the procession of boats wind its way from Shilshole Bay inland to Lake Washington.

The F/V (fishing vessel) *Seymour* from 1913 is one of the dozen or so historic halibut schooners still working from Ballard. Originally, there were over 130 halibut schooners in the fleet; sails supplemented the power of two-cylinder gas engines, and crew fished from small dories that were launched over the side into the dangerous North Pacific waters. Today, these schooners commonly use diesel, and the dories are long gone. Like Ballard, these vessels have stood the test of time, evolving and maturing but remaining rooted in history and tradition.

From longlining to seining, commercial fishing has long been an integral part of Ballard's economy and culture. During the period from just before World War I to just after World War II, the mechanization of fishing gear transformed the fishing industry. Originally, men would fish from small vessels. The dories would be taken out to the deep-sea fishing grounds on the decks of large steamboats or sail/motor-power boats and dropped over the side. With mechanization came combination boats that could be rigged for different varieties of fishing. Mechanization also allowed for smaller crews and access to distant fishing grounds. The 1906 photograph above is of the F/V *San Juan*, its crew, and its cod catch.

In this photograph the F/V *Ethel* is docked at Fishermen's Terminal around 1950. Note the fisherman in the background using a fire hydrant to assist with his net work.

This photograph shows fishermen mending nets at the net yard at Fishermen's Terminal. Originally attracting immigrants from Scandinavia and then Eastern Europe, Ballard welcomed people who brought with them fishing traditions and techniques from all over the world. Ballard's fishing industry has contributed billions of dollars to Ballard's economy, and Ballard remains a hub of the North American fishing industry today. (Courtesy of MOHAI.)

This 1940s photograph shows women cleaning fish at a fish processing plant. The *Seattle Weekly News* reported in November 1930 that 200 of the 300 boats in the North Pacific halibut fleet were from Ballard. The Depression had a huge effect on the local and national economy; many industries never recovered. But the fishing industry survived with the help of tax relief passed by the state legislature.

The halibut schooner *H.B. Jones* was built for Capt. Charles White in 1910 at Cooke & Lake in Ballard. The Cooke & Lake yard was located just east of where the locks are today, one of many shipyards crowded along the beach among the mills and other industry. William Lake, of Cooke & Lake, was one of the sons of T.W. Lake, a famous early Ballard shipbuilder from Norway. The elder Lake had built boats in Ballard as early as 1871. The *H.B. Jones* was one of dozens of halibut schooners built and based in Ballard. She is pictured here at the downtown waterfront, where she likely came to sell her catch.

This c. 1909 photograph shows the *Viking*, built by Sievert E. Sagstad of Ballard for Norway Day during the Alaska-Yukon-Pacific Exposition (AYPE). The replica of a Viking ship was sailed from the north end of Lake Washington to Portage Bay during the exposition. In 2009, the Nordic Heritage Museum renovated an antique hull called the *Nordic Spirit* to replicate the Vikings' crossing during the 100th anniversary celebration of the AYPE. The *Nordic Spirit* made its debut (on wheels) as part of the 17th of May Parade. (Courtesy of MOHAI.)

THE SHINGLE 1948

The *Shingle* has been Ballard High School's yearbook almost since its first graduating class of 1902, which had only four students. In 1907, Ballard High School became part of Seattle Public Schools, but its yearbook covers always drew inspiration from the community. This 1948 cover features a fisherman prepared for foul weather, with a troller on the horizon. The high school offers the interdisciplinary Maritime Academy unique to Seattle.

Ballard Oil is one many proud supporters of the maritime industry, supplying oil to fishing fleets from a waterfront location and by truck to homeowners. The fourth generation of Aakerviks run this business, established in 1937. Their Shilshole neighbor Salmon Bay Sand & Gravel has become one of the Northwest's largest suppliers of construction materials; founded in the year of annexation, 1907, it is run by the fourth generation of the Nerdrum family. (Above, courtesy of Ballard Oil; below, courtesy of Abby Inpanbutr.)

Bowie Electric trucks have changed since this c. 1975 picture, but the company remains a familiar presence in Ballard. Founded in 1916 and a longtime fixture on Ballard Avenue, Fred Hoefer purchased the business in 1947. The family-owned business has provided electrical contracting services for over 100 years. (Courtesy of Seattle Municipal Archives.)

The *Republic* is a 75-foot wood schooner built at Fishing Vessel Owners Marine Ways (FVO) at Fishermen's Terminal around 1893. Part of the halibut fleet, there were roughly 125 boats operating from a single port. The *Republic* is still plying the waters of Alaska. (Courtesy of Abby Inpanbutr.)

There has been a shipyard on this site at the base on Twenty-fourth Avenue NW since 1871, well before Ballard's incorporation. The Lake Shipyard was briefly a lumber mill but has had a rich and storied history as a shipyard since 1902, building a variety of stern-wheelers and minesweepers, one of which became Cousteau's R/V *Calypso*. Located by the Ballard Marine Railroad as Pacific Fishermen Company, the shipyard flourished after World War II when it became owned and operated by some 400 Norwegian fishermen. The shipyard has also become a final resting place for iconic Ballard and Seattle signage. (Courtesy of Abby Inpanbutr.)

As a longtime liveaboard, the writer Jay Craig has witnessed Ballard businesses, maritime and otherwise, from a different vantage point. This compilation of signage, past and present, is also a nod to the collection of the originals that are housed at Pacific Fishermen Shipyard. (Courtesy of Jay Craig.)

Ballard is a maritime place. Big and small boats alike have always been used for numerous tasks along Ballard's waterways. The Shilshole Indians utilized both saltwater and river canoes to hunt and fish and as daily transportation. Later, the Mosquito Fleet transported people, goods, and mail from port to port around the region. For some decades, a ferry used to run from Ballard to Port Ludlow from a ferry terminal located where Ray's Boathouse is today. During Prohibition years, there was a small fleet of boats in Ballard used by local rumrunners. Currently, working and pleasure craft are constantly going to and from the Puget Sound to the ship canal through the locks.

August Werner designed this impressive statue of Leif Erikson, which was presented to the Port of Seattle at the world's fair in 1962. Today, Leif staunchly stares toward the Salish Sea surrounded by a ship-shaped circle of stones bearing the names of Nordic immigrants. The masts of Shilshole Bay Marina, built by the port in 1962, are in the background of this photograph. An active liveaboard community, the largest on the West Coast, resides here in some of the thousand-plus pleasure and commercial craft moored at the marina. (Courtesy of Laura K. Cooper.)

This magnificent sculpture has bronze name plaques at its base honoring more than 675 local commercial fishermen and women who have lost their lives while at sea since the turn of the 20th century. The memorial was made possible by years of effort and contributions from Seattle's commercial fishing community. Located near the docks at Fishermen's Terminal since 1988, the memorial provides a place for remembrance. (Courtesy of Tod Gangler.)

Three

BALLARD'S BEAT

Ballard Avenue was Ballard's first downtown core, and despite varying fortunes, it never lost its essential importance. Challenged during Prohibition and the decline of the mills, it seemed frozen in the 1940s. This appearance was key in the bid to make Ballard Avenue one of just eight Historic Landmark Districts in the city of Seattle. That recognition and preservation effort has become key to its resurgent popularity at all hours of the day.

Only a block from the Ballard's two earliest industries located on the waterfront, shingle milling and boatbuilding, a bustling commercial district developed along Ballard Avenue. In addition to dry good stores, Ballard Avenue housed most of Ballard's saloons. An early description said Ballard Avenue was "four blocks with 27 saloons." Over time, and perhaps because of its bars and nightlife, Ballard Avenue became known for its music scene, with venues that have continuously served Ballard, even if the names have changed. For example, Conor Byrne Pub, Tractor Tavern, and Sunset Tavern are all located where the first saloons and taverns operated between retailers and manufacturers. "One of Seattle's oldest running watering holes nestled in the historical heart of Ballard" is how Conor Byrne Pub bills itself, proving that Ballard Avenue never lost its beat.

Even though the commercial center of Ballard shifted away from Ballard Avenue to Northwest Market Street (or simply Market Street) in the late 1920s and 1930s, in part due to Prohibition, Ballard Avenue has remained a lifeline to the heart of Ballard's independent businesses and a hot spot for drinking and dining, shopping, and entertainment. Its buildings are listed in the National Register of Historic Places thanks to the efforts of local residents who anticipated its potential destruction in the 1970s. Ballard's former town hall bell rings on the hour and to open and close the weekly Ballard Farmers Market. Today, both Ballard Avenue and Market Street form the nexus of downtown Ballard.

In a 1988 oral history, Ballardite and musician Ray Denend remembered accompanying his musician parents to play at the many dance halls in Ballard. As he became a musician with his own band, he recalled the nightlife of the 1930s "playing for the kitty," which could mean coins left in a dish or, later on, free beer. He recalls when beer was 10¢ a glass. It was not only the fishermen who were thirsty.

This photograph depicts early Ballard Avenue with its dirt road, wooden sidewalks, and streetcar rail. In 1904, approximately $140,000 was slated to be spent on creating cement walks, brick street paving, and sewer work. Private litigants had sued the city for injuries suffered on the wood planking shown here. The massive improvements along Ballard Avenue around the turn of the 20th century had a stimulating effect on land values and rents. Lots along Ballard Avenue soared and sold for between $2,000 and $5,000. Rents ranged between $75 and $100 for a storefront and $10 to $15 for an office space.

Looking north to Ballard City Hall in the distance, this photograph documents early road construction along Ballard Avenue. Wooden planks were used to replace dirt roads as wood was abundant. Eventually, the planks were replaced with brick and stone and then pavement.

Ballard Ave –looking north–

Ballard's population tripled from its incorporation in 1890 (1,636 residents) to 1900 (4,568 residents) and tripled again by 1910 (16,128 residents). Ballard Avenue was the center of it all. This photograph depicts recently improved Ballard Avenue with bricks and trolley tracks. Ballard City Hall, seen prominently at the end upper end of Ballard Avenue, was built in 1899.

Note the sign in the picture, "Bartell Drug Store No. 4." Bartell Drug Company started in Seattle in 1890 and was the longest-running chain of independent drugstores in the country until its sale in 2020. This postcard of Ballard Avenue went from Ferd to Sophia Svendsen in Kristiansund, Northern Norway. In Norwegian, it reads as follows: "I am sending you a card of a street in the town where I live. I will also send you a letter. Today is one of those long sad Sundays with rain and winds so that one cannot go anywhere." It was mailed on November 21, 1910, for the cost of 2¢.

As the first municipality to incorporate after Washington achieved statehood in 1890, Ballard has (almost) always had its iconic bell. Ballard City Hall, at the triangular intersection of Ballard Avenue and Twenty-second Avenue NW, was the focal point of the business district and its civic home beginning in 1899. It housed the police force, fire department, jail, and public offices and had a dance floor. On top was a bell tower, with a bell that signaled shift changes for the mill workers, public emergencies, and a 9:00 p.m. curfew for children. Draped in black crepe, it also tolled Ballard's annexation to Seattle in May 1907. Ballard's expanding population increased the demands on law enforcement. A report for January 1 to September 30, 1894, revealed that the police provided charitable help, made arrests, and collected fines. The 203 arrests during the six months ranged from drunk and disorderly conduct to attempting to debauch public morals. Ballard's city hall graced one end of Ballard Avenue. Its jailhouse was called the "Ballard Hotel" because of the large number of men allowed to sleep there on cold, rainy nights. (Courtesy of Seattle Municipal Archives.)

A 1965 earthquake led to the eventual end of Ballard's city hall. The 1,000-pound bell went north to the former grounds of Firland Sanitarium. However, retired state senator Ted Peterson and several other local leaders never gave up on the bell's rightful return. The bell was returned to Ballard in 1976 and temporarily resided at the locks. In 1988, the Centennial Bell Committee, thanks to its fundraising efforts, resurrected the bell in a new tower at the original location. The dedication also celebrated Ballard Avenue as one of the city of Seattle's landmark districts. One important part of the restoration project remained incomplete—a mechanism to automate the ringing of the bell. In 2011, the Ballard Historical Society won a Seattle Small & Simple grant and was able to fulfill the dream of the Centennial Bell Committee and "Bring the Ring Back to Ballard." The Ballard Bell tolls daily on the hour and anchors the weekly Ballard Farmers Market and is a meeting place and destination. (Courtesy of Laura K. Cooper.)

Tacoma residents James and Welthia Kelsey constructed this one-story building in 1903 as an investment. They entered into an agreement with Eugene Felt, the owner of the Felt Block next door, to create an internal opening between their two buildings, which accommodated additional retail space. A shadow of the original archway is still visible on an interior wall. The ground-level exterior initially opened to the street, providing open-air service for Bruce Armstrong's Dry Goods Store. During the 1930s, it was home to the Pioneer Clothing Store. Olsen Furniture took up residence here in the early 1940s and furnished Ballard (and beyond) homes for over three quarters of century.

In 1920, Charles and Edna Halverson built this structure to house their ladies and gents furnishings store, which they ran successfully for 34 years. Shortly after opening, they expanded their retail focus to include dry goods. During the late 1940s, they renamed their business the Ballard Department Store, a name it retained until closing in 1955.

The Scandinavian American Bank's Ballard branch operated from this Second Empire Baroque structure since its construction in 1902 until the bank failed in 1921 and the building was taken over by the Canal Bank, later a Seattle First National Bank (1924–1932). The building in recent years has been the Starlight Hotel and now Ballard Inn. Incorporated in 1892, the bank's main branch was at the southwest corner of Yesler Way and First Avenue and boasted of a capital listed at $75,000. It was founded by the Seattle capitalist and civic leader Andrew Chilberg, who was also a founder of the Seattle Swedish Club and vice consul for Sweden and Norway. Chilberg was a founding board member of Swedish Hospital in 1910, and his bank financed its operations.

Arthur Bourgett, president of the Motor Shingle Company, built this Romanesque Revival structure in 1901 to house the Motor Bar, which he owned until his death in 1905. The bar continued to operate under different owners until Leland Salinger opened a men's furnishings store for three years beginning in 1907. In 1912, Bartell Drug Store No. 4 moved into this location, with Ballard pioneer pharmacist Arthur Preston as the manager. With the start of the Depression, Bartell followed the commercial exodus from Ballard Avenue to Northwest Market Street.

Constructed by Seattle saloon owner Stephano Raggio in 1904, the Junction Building originally stood three stories tall with a crenellated turret. Unfortunately, fire destroyed the third floor, requiring its removal. In the early 1900s, the ground floor was occupied by the Junction Saloon. In 1910, the Crystal Theater opened, entertaining the public with moving pictures and performances until 1915. Initially, the upper levels provided office space for physicians and attorneys, including H.E. Peck, one-time Ballard mayor. In later years, this space became the Junction Apartments, with a bank on the ground floor. Currently, the ground floor has returned to its food-and-drink roots.

Brothers Charles and Richard Kutzner built the Queen Hotel, located on the right side of this photograph. Their successful barber business in downtown Seattle provided sufficient capital to build the Kutzner Block on Ballard Avenue in 1904. In early February 1916, a record 38 inches of snow fell on Ballard. This snowstorm resulted in the closure of all transportation routes to Seattle. However, this did not stop the citizens of Ballard. Being of resourceful pioneer stock, many residents boarded their boats and traveled to work via the newly opened Ballard Locks.

Small shops long occupied the ground floor of the Princess Hotel building. The name confers a grandeur that was not matched by the rooms rented upstairs by fishermen and mill workers.

Formerly located at 4833 Ballard Avenue, the Fern Café was in the heart of the Ballard Avenue business district. Saloons lined both sides of the street until 1916. In 1916, Washington became a dry state and remained so for the next 16 years. Where once free lunches had been served to encourage the sale of beer and whiskey, liquor establishments were converted to full-time cafés.

Through the 1890s, this was the most imposing structure in Ballard. William Cors and Robert Wegener were proprietors of the Ballard Wine House. These two men first became business associates in 1889 and opened the Ballard Wine House a year later in a wooden building at this location. In 1893, they constructed this impressive structure to house their thriving business. Cors and Wegener were once described as "artists in compound mixtures and fancy beverages." They even provided a separate entrance and private room for women. The *Ballard News*, a local newspaper run by J.D. Ruffner & Sons, had office space in the building as early as 1904.

This 1908 structure cost just $15,000 to build as the Fitzgerald & Hynes Department Store. The Ballard Aerie of Eagles leased the two upper floors, followed by Willy's New Car Sales & Dealership. In the 1950s, the *Ballard News Tribune* printed newspapers from its presses on the second floor. In her 1988 oral history, Kitty Grace Crawford recalled working for the paper from 1946 to 1974. This included the year when the *Ballard News* and the *Ballard Tribune* were combined in 1963. The publishing company was owned by the Kimballs, who also lived on the third floor of the building. The building was only a block south of Northwest Market Street, but Crawford recalled, "You might as just as well be five miles away because I never got up there." A coworker who went to a lunchroom near the office would come back with gossip to spare about doings on Ballard Avenue.

The Matthes brothers built this entire block. Its brick northern corner is beautifully preserved. Home to a long-standing health club and now an adjoining hotel, the building has housed a saloon, a bank, a post office, and the Elks Hall and is rumored to have been a speakeasy and cardroom during Prohibition. In a nod to its past, the interior features large prints from the Ballard Historical Society's photographic archives.

Longtime Ballard bar owner Charley Swanson built this structure in 1904 and opened the Owl Saloon here with his partner Leonard Strygen. Except for the years during Prohibition, when the Owl Café occupied the ground floor, this building has continuously housed a tavern. The Owl remained in operation under that name until 1993, when Conor Byrne bought it and changed the name. The pub has changed hands a few times since then but is still located there, proud of its place in the heart of historic Ballard.

Prior to Ballard's annexation to Seattle in 1907, Seattle's mayor and city council began to crack down on Seattle's liquor establishments. The laws reduced the hours for liquor sales and required Sunday closures. The changes in Seattle's saloon regulations made the more liberal town of Ballard even more popular. The standard crowd from Ballard was joined by Seattle's weekend drinkers who found their way over the bridge in search of a friendlier place to spend their Sundays. Ballard enacted the same laws, but the local government refused to enforce them in favor of supporting the saloon owners' rights to do business. Instead, they passed a resolution to have Seattle's City Light put cattle cars on the streetcar lines for removing the Seattle drunks. (Below, courtesy of National Nordic Museum.)

Formed in 1912, the Deep Sea Fishermen's Union of the Pacific, referred to by friends as DSFU, was created by workingmen on Seattle's waterfront who sought practical goals—higher wages and safer working conditions. In addition to labor concerns, fishing conservation has been part of their ongoing advocacy over the last years. Look for their hook at 5215 Ballard Avenue NW, a building that dates back to 1902 and is one of the most historically significant structures on the landmarked avenue. (Courtesy of Deep Sea Fishermen's Union.)

Bridging the maritime history and that of Ballard's literal beat, the Tractor Tavern is also located in the ground-floor space of the Deep Sea Fishermen's Union building. There has almost always been an entertainment venue in this location, from Scandinavian dance hall to concert venues, both before and after DSFU acquired the building in 1948. Perhaps the New Melody Tavern was its best-known incarnation before the Tractor began rocking the music scene in the early 1990s; whether through zydeco, country, or alternative rock, being eclectic is part of what has made it enduring and essential to Ballard Avenue's reemergence as a music mecca. (Courtesy of Laura K. Cooper.)

"Ballard's Last Stand Since 1904" is how Hattie's Hat describes itself. It has been serving three meals a day at the bar and booths in front and Aunt Harriet's room in the back. Over the front door, it says, "Cocktails," which has made it a destination its entire history. Originally the Old Home, it is said that hard-drinking could describe every incarnation. There is a Scandinavian mural by Fred Oldfield (restored in 1997) that has seen it all by now. Hattie's Hat lives on. (Courtesy of Seattle Municipal Archives.)

Any place calling itself a smoke shop will attract a certain clientele, and this regular looks right at home. Ballard Smoke Shop, the Sunset, and Hattie's Hat—all of these Ballard Avenue establishments have played musical chairs along the avenue, with the Sunset at one point moving to where Ballard's first Chinese restaurant, the Chung Sun, was located. The venues are now united through the ownership of a man who believes in preserving bars of the past, right down to original menus. However, there is no more smoking in the Smoke Shop. (Right, courtesy of Don Wallen Collection, University of Washington Special Collections; below, courtesy of Seattle Municipal Archives.)

Initially a side street to Ballard Avenue, Market Street became the heart of the Ballard commercial district in the 1930s, aided by an extension on the east side to Phinney Ridge and on the west side to Golden Gardens. This early picture of Market Street shows that it was originally a residential street. When Ballard was platted, Market Street (originally called Broadway) was positioned as far south as it was possible to have a street with a straight east-west orientation given Ballard's curved shoreline.

When Market Street began its transition from residential to business, this Second Renaissance Revival–style building made for a grand corner. It was constructed by the Fraternal Order of Eagles; stories within its 100-year-old walls could fuel an ongoing series. The Bagdad Theater occupied the lower level for three decades. Ballard Accident and General Hospital was on the third floor from 1928 to 1954. Lafferty's Drug on the corner offered prescription service and a lunch counter. Later, there were restaurants in the corner space, while offices above were still a warren of jewelers, accountants, attorneys, and now therapists. Even before an addition that includes a rooftop penthouse, the Ballard Building created one-of-a-kind memories for those who attended concerts in the Backstage Nightclub. The kitchen is rumored to have been a hospital morgue, and its swinging doors later gave way to part of an exercise room in the Ballard Health Club, established 1988.

Four

BUILDING BALLARD

Ballard's growth has always been dictated by real estate development. The original "real estate developers" of Ballard, John Leary and William Ballard, laid out and incorporated Ballard in 1889. Plat maps of Ballard were recorded in June 1889, just a week before Seattle was ablaze in the great Seattle fire. The fire provided an opportunity for mills along Salmon Bay to supply construction materials.

After annexation, Ballard was billed as being "just 20 minutes from downtown." Bridges, roads, streetcars, and buses were all eventually built to allow access to and from Ballard, and the treed landscape gave way to platted lots for residential housing. Ballard's housing stock grew as Ballard consistently topped all other Seattle neighborhoods for pre–World War II growth.

Early Ballard houses were often farmhouses with room for large gardens, which were later infilled with more houses. Single-family lots, measuring 50 feet by 100 feet, were actually double plats so that each lot was allowed to have two houses. This explains Ballard's eclectic housing styles with Victorians next to postwar boxes; although a few streets do have consistent architectural styles in a row. Today, in Ballard, there are still pioneer farmhouses, company (mill) cottages, Victorian, Classic Box, Craftsman/Bungalows, and Tudor Revival styles. Ballard also has a plethora of Mid-Century Minimalist homes, most often called Mench (named for the building contractor), and a healthy miscellany as original lots were divided and developed after World War II.

In the 1990s, the concept of creating urban villages throughout Seattle attempted to concentrate growth near commercial districts and prevent sprawl. By 2015, Ballard had exceeded predicted population growth by over 300 percent. Houses in the up-zoned residential area designated as the urban village core and newly up-zoned areas outside of the original urban village designation are being replaced with apartment buildings and town houses at a rapid rate.

In 2014, the Ballard Historical Society (BHS) won a grant from the City of Seattle to inventory and map the existing pre-1950 structures and assess them for architectural integrity. Over 100 trained volunteers mapped nearly 7,000 structures and exceptional trees to create a snapshot of past Ballard in the present day. This Mapping Historic Ballard project led to the inclusion of more historic designations for buildings and historical research on 160 structures. As part of its mission to preserve and celebrate Ballard, BHS presents a classic home tour every three years.

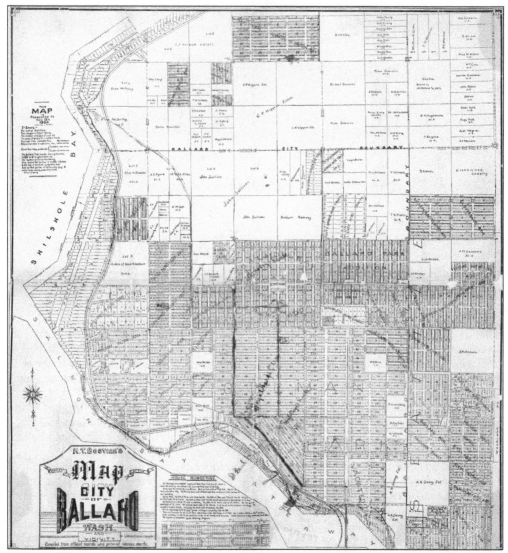

This 1904 map of the city shows what Ballard looked like before annexation. At the time, Ballard's northern boundary was Eighty-fifth Street NW. The eastern boundary was Eighth Avenue NW, named Division; however, now, Third Avenue NW is the eastern border. Its western border was present-day Thirty-second Avenue NW, and beyond was called Ballard Station heading down to Puget Sound. Its southern border has always been the ship canal. Note there is little development north of Sixty-fifth Street, which was called Ship Street. (Courtesy of MOHAI.)

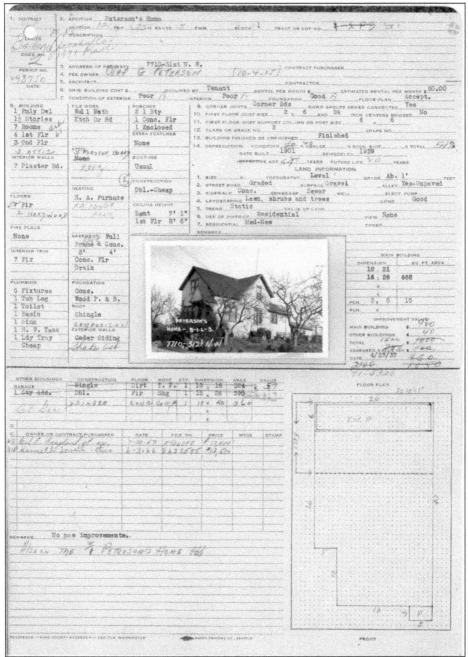

Historical research is greatly aided by archives maintained by Puget Sound Regional Archives, Seattle Municipal, Museum of History and Industry, University of Washington, and Special Collections at the Seattle Public Library. Between side sewer cards and old property record cards much information can be gleaned. As in this example, there is often a photograph, sketch of the exterior plan, and information about the owner and amenities. Many of the photographs of pre–World War II houses in Seattle were part of a Works Progress Administration (WPA) project in the 1930s that employed photographers to document every residence and building in Seattle. (Courtesy of Puget Sound Regional Archives.)

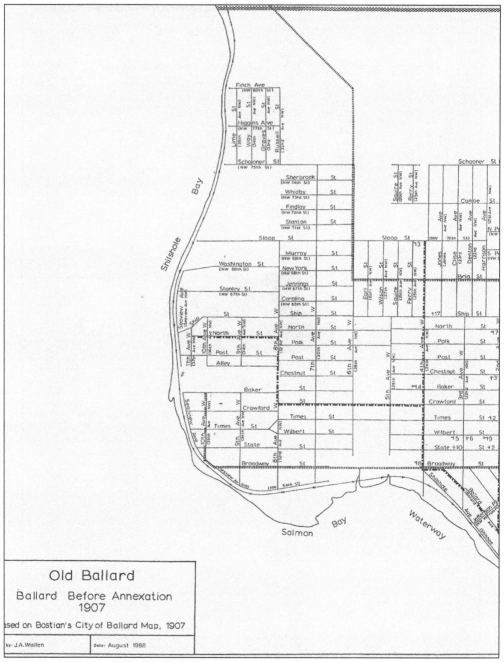

This map shows that Ballard had different street names when it was an independent town. After annexation, Ballard's street names were changed to conform to Seattle's nomenclature: Ship Street was renamed Sixty-fifth Street NW and Main Street became Fifteenth Avenue NW.

Streets that did not coordinate with the Seattle street grid maintained their original names, such as Mary, Alonzo, Tallman, and Shilshole Avenues. Today, some of the original street names can be seen at certain corners, inlaid in blue-and-white tile in the sidewalk.

This 1917 picture of the Ballard Bridge was taken on opening day. The original Ballard Bridge was constructed in 1889, providing the first-ever direct access to Seattle from Ballard. A tiny island originally stood in the bridge's current location. Anchored to this island (at the turn of the century) was a pest house. Built initially upon a scow and, eventually, secured to the island with pilings, the pest house was used as a quarantine facility during epidemics of diphtheria, scarlet fever, smallpox, and polio. (Courtesy of Seattle Municipal Archives.)

This 1920s photograph of the Ballard Bridge shows that it was built as a double bascule bridge with wooden approaches. The current Ballard Bridge has the original bascule mechanism; steel and cement replaced the wooden approaches in 1940 with funding from the Works Progress Administration. (Courtesy of MOHAI.)

In 1890, the first streetcar started operating in Ballard. Twelve motorized streetcars made two daily trips. The cost of a ride was 5¢, with a transfer, and the streetcar collected about $20 a day. In 1902, the Fremont-Ballard Streetcar began service. People could live in Ballard and easily commute to downtown Seattle every day. Unfortunately, streetcars were unreliable and often overcrowded. Ballard's streetcar system started to decline in the 1930s, and the last Ballard streetcar run ended in 1941. The City of Seattle replaced the electric streetcars with diesel buses and trackless trolleys.

Ballard is separated from Seattle by the Salmon Bay waterway. Ballard's transportation infrastructure was, and still is, an ongoing issue. Due to its proximity to water, boats were an important form of transport when Ballard was founded. Ballard's first bridge was built in 1889, and the first railroad bridge went up in 1890. Ballard had its own stop on the railroad. In 1890, the private trolley company, the West Street Electric Company, initiated trains between Ballard and Seattle. Eventually, the trolley track network through Ballard was extensive. Traces of these tracks can still be seen on some roads in Ballard today and explain why some streets in Ballard are much wider.

Ballard was a working-class city, and many of the homes in Ballard are modest compared with other parts of Seattle. Wood was abundant and cheap. Many of Ballard's older homes are built from old growth timber, superior in quality to second growth or farmed lumber. This photograph shows the home of an early Norwegian immigrant, which was undoubtedly replaced with a more substantial house. (Courtesy of the National Nordic Museum.)

Postcards of private homes were prevalent in early Ballard, as they were around the Puget Sound. Photographers would travel around and take pictures of people at their homes and then turn these pictures into postcards for mailing.

This section of land located in Salmon Bay was originally platted as Gilman Park in 1888. Old notes identify the street as what is now called Twenty-second Avenue NW. When Gilman Park was divided into lots by the West Coast Improvement Company, standard lots were 50 feet by 100 feet and varied in price from $75 to $240. Two of Ballard's many builders stand at a construction site below.

This appealing Folk Victorian–style farmhouse was built in 1905 when Ballard was still a city and touted as the "Shingle Capital of the World." Preservation-minded homeowners were thrilled to find an original building receipt in a doorjamb during their restoration. This home was built for the offspring of the pioneer family of Rev. Eli T. Hamblet, namesake of the Hamblet's Acre Gardens.

This quaint Victorian gives one the impression of a miniature mansion. With nine-foot ceilings, this modest floor plan offers grandeur on a small scale. Property records of 1922 indicate this house was rented for $15 a month. Typical of Ballard, this house represents the lasting functionality and livability of older, well-built homes.

Listed in the Washington State Register of Historic Places since 1998, the home is called Baker Street House for the street name when it was built in 1888. The home recently survived threat of being moved as the block was rezoned to allow a mix of townhouses. Its neighbors have changed, but the home's current placement has been preserved. (Courtesy of Puget Sound Regional Archives.)

Only a handful of houses were built in the 19th century in Ballard, and this quaint old Victorian home is one of them. This house exemplifies lasting craftsmanship.

This stately 1911 Craftsman was built high above the street and maintains stunning territorial views. The exterior has a porch, chimney, and foundation built of granite and sandstone. The builder was a stonemason who reportedly constructed the Theodore Jacobsen Observatory at the University of Washington and used leftover stones to build his home.

Ballard benefitted immensely from an influx of skilled, hardworking European tradesman in the early 20th century. Built in 1913, this handsome Craftsman stands as a testament to old Ballard's modest, yet finely crafted homes, still enjoyed and appreciated today.

In 1914, Dr. Ferdinand A. Christensen had this home built for both his family and his medical practice. The home's design included an office and an examination room. Christensen was a tuberculosis doctor and was said to have housed patients in the upper sleeping porch. While Craftsman bungalows proliferated in Ballard in the early 20th century, this home's larger size and rich detail set it apart.

John Kastner made a point of having features that set his home apart. In 1914, he built this impressive Craftsman on the streetcar line. The robust clinker brick front porch supports columns of cement and gravel with a unique low-relief decoration. The massive front door leads into a living room rich with beautiful fir millwork.

Unique to Ballard and Seattle, this 1906 Swiss Chalet Revival–style house was built by John W. Dorman. Capitalizing on his good fortune as manager of the Stimson Mill, he built this ornately grand house on Sunset Hill, sparing no expense or decoration. In 1978, thoughtful owners James and Hazel Norvell achieved national landmark status in order to preserve this impressive house. Locals know it as Norvell House because the owners lived there from 1949 to 2005.

In 1907, Frank Hinman Waskey had this home built for his family as a warm alternative to living in Alaska. They built this plantation-style home with an expansive wraparound porch so their children could play outside in any weather. Situated high above the streetcar line, this home was later nicknamed the "Ferry House." For years, it was painted white with green trim; these colors made the home look like a Washington state ferry.

This castle-like Spanish Revival house was built in 1930 and has retained its architectural integrity. It was Isak and Jakobina Johnson's first home after they emigrated from Iceland. They later lived in the Sobey House and raised seven children. (Courtesy of Puget Sound Regional Archives.)

This whimsical Storybook-style late-Craftsman house with its dramatic full-pitch roofline and massive stone chimney is a one-of-a-kind Ballard home. In 1936, Emil Petersen began work on this charming house. He and his wife, Vollea, collected stones from the area for the chimney. Emil, a skilled artist, painted the interior rosemaling floral decorations in the traditional Norwegian folk style.

Increasingly obscured by foliage but always evoking curiosity, this 1905 Foursquare sits on a Sunset Hill corner. It was built by the owner of Sobey Manufacturing Company, James Sobey, and his wife, Besse, both influential locals. Sobey died in 1930, and the home was later sold to Icelanders Isak and Jakobina Johnson. Jakobina made a name for herself as a poetess and translator. She was awarded the Order of the Falcons by the king of Denmark. With its multipaned windows and wraparound porch, the home appears untouched in decades. It is still owned by a Johnson (by marriage), making it a rare Ballard home to be owned by only two families, though multiple generations. (Courtesy of Puget Sound Regional Archives.)

Built around 1908, this American Foursquare used a Sears floor plan. On a larger scale than most houses in Ballard, this beauty sits prominently on a corner lot. Graceful and stately, the house has hosted generations of families through its long life.

The brick Tudor Revival style has long been popular in Ballard and often features oak floors with mahogany inlay design. This lovely 1936 house has all the Tudor-style bells and whistles. Arched doorways, coved ceilings, stucco walls, and elegant lead glass windows are present inside. These sturdy, charming houses are found throughout Ballard.

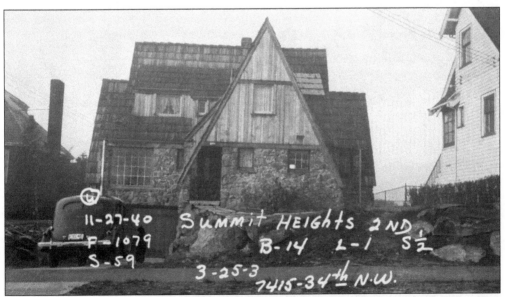

In 1940, this house was built on the Sunset Hill bluff on land formerly owned by the Great Northern Railroad. This Storybook-style Tudor with its steep roofline and rugged half-timbering is enhanced by a variety of textures inside and out. Warm pine interior walls as well as the oak hardwood floors and box beam ceilings add a cabin-like feel.

This charming home, built in late 1941, is a fine example of a typical Mench design. Earl F. Mench was a prolific builder and developer of homes in north Ballard between the Great Depression and before the end of World War II. Characteristic features of Mench houses include a tall chimney in the middle of the front, a small portal window near the front door, windows with horizontally divided wood panes, and wood lintels over the doors and windows. Carefully preserved and restored to its original 1940s character, this home reflects the excellent craftsmanship, quality of materials, and attention to detail that distinguish Mench houses.

Here is a typical mid-century house with a Norwegian flag flying proudly and a Ballard driver clearly nearby. (Courtesy of Abby Inpanbutr.)

New apartments in Ballard boast of mixed-use retail, but that has long been the case here. At right is Manning's first Ballard location on the street level with law offices upstairs. Below is a multifamily dwelling at Fifteenth Avenue NW, dating to 1927, that has always had small business owners at the street level. (Right, courtesy of Seattle Municipal Archives; below, courtesy of Puget Sound Regional Archives.)

The brick retail building on the pointy corner of Northwest Eighty-fifth Street and Thirty-second Avenue NW was built in 1928 and is seen at the top of the road and stairs leading down to Golden Gardens. For 34 years, from 1939 to 1973, the space housed neighborhood grocers or druggists, including Lee Quality Food, Hoefer's Market, and Smitty's and Ethel's Beauty Palor.

The 1960s and 1970s brought change even to the sleepy corner of Sunset Hill. A University District business known as a "head shop" for its marijuana paraphernalia moved to this intersection. They also sold records, tapes, and its own type of accessories. Now home to a coffee shop and restaurant, this unofficial Ballard boundary location is a popular neighborhood spot.

Old growth wood was used to construct this 1890 small frame church. Built for the German Evangelical Church, it currently houses the Interfaith Community Sanctuary. The interior has its original wood wainscoting and straight grain fir flooring. It has been used as a schoolhouse as well as a church. It was designated a landmark in 1980 by the Seattle Preservation Board. (Courtesy of Puget Sound Regional Archives.)

A large number of buildings were constructed as churches in the sector just north of downtown Ballard up to Northwest Sixty-fifth Street. Although not all are still in use for religious purposes, the collection includes wooden churches that are distinctive within Seattle as a whole.

Sunset Hill Community Club was built in 1929 in the Jennings Ballard Addition. It was a highly influential representative of the many such neighborhood civic improvement clubs stemming from the late 1910s and 1920s, and the building (along with Bitter Lake, and Seward Park buildings) is among the few that survive. This civic space has hosted thousands of events over the last century, from its Friday night dances to voting stations. Available for rental, the lovely upstairs has a stage, while the basement level has a full kitchen. The building was remodeled in 1999 through community fundraising and a matching city grant. The club has always fostered community engagement and is the longest-running community club in Seattle. (Courtesy of Seattle Municipal Archives.)

Founded on May 13, 1903, the Leif Erikson Sons of Norway Lodge is the oldest Sons of Norway lodge on the West Coast. The current location in Ballard was constructed in 1986, but over its history, the lodge built three headquarters: Norway Hall, on Boren Avenue, now a Seattle landmark; Norway Center, in downtown Seattle, which was purchased by the Mountaineers and later demolished; and the present Leif Erikson Hall in Ballard. The fraternal organization, though originally for men only, has admitted women since 1927. It serves local members of Norwegian birth and descent with health benefits, life insurance, financial and social services, and recreational programs. The lodge offers a monthly "Kaffestua" and special events, such as Norwegian Cultural and Heritage Day in March, a Leif to Leif Fun Run/Walk (between the lodge and the Leif Erikson Statue at Shilshole Bay Marina), and an annual fall bazaar. (Courtesy of Laura K. Cooper.)

The second-grade class of Webster Elementary School, located at 3014 Northwest Sixty-seventh Street, poses next to the school in 1916. Constructed in 1908, Webster served as an elementary school for children in Ballard through 1979. From 1979 to 2018, the Nordic Heritage Museum leased the building, which housed exhibitions and events showcasing Nordic American culture. The Seattle Landmarks Preservation Board designated both building and site as historical landmarks. (Courtesy of National Nordic Museum.)

The Nordic Heritage Museum began leasing the building after low enrollment in the 1970s forced the closure of the school. Today, the museum has a new home at 2655 Northwest Market Street, the previous location of the Fenpro Building. A growing young population in Ballard has prompted the reopening of Webster School, now with modern renovations. (Courtesy of the National Nordic Museum.)

After nearly 40 years in the leased Webster School, the Nordic Heritage Museum moved into a new home in the heart of Ballard, at 2655 Northwest Market Street. With the new location came a new name and a national designation—the National Nordic Museum. Designed by Mithun Architects, the block-long exterior of the building is of minimalist construction and framed by plants native to both the Pacific Northwest and the Nordic countries. The interior architecture is based around the theme of a fjord, which includes bridges linking together the stories and people of the European homeland and the Americas. The new museum serves not only as a home to more than 80,000 objects, but also as a community gathering place, with dining, concerts, lectures, and other educational programs. Below shows the opening ceremony of the museum in 2018 with dignitaries from all five Nordic countries in attendance. (Above, courtesy of Abby Inpanbutr; below, courtesy of Laura K. Cooper.)

This is an "old-style" lumberyard, such as used to be common in Ballard. Located on Market Street, Limback is a family-owned business, now run by the third generation and approaching its ninth decade. The framing lumber is kiln-dried Douglas fir, and the lumberyard is known for having an excellent inventory of cedar, finishing lumber, and mouldings. (Courtesy of Laura K. Cooper.)

When this 1902 Victorian beauty near industrial Ballard went up for sale, classic home lovers worried. Instead, the new owners have restored its original elegance. Meanwhile longtime next-door owners demolished and started from scratch in 2017, showing how old and new can coexist. (Courtesy of Davidya Kasperzyk.)

Five

BEHOLD BALLARD

Ballard attracted a large immigrant population. Scandinavians, in particular, migrated to the area because logging and fishing were familiar industries, and the region's landscape reminded them of their origins but with a better growing climate.

Ballard's maritime climate was good for dairy farming and growing fruit. The occasional gnarled fruit tree can still be seen in some residential yards left from orchards of the past. Just north of the Ballard city limit of Eighty-fifth Street, the lots tend to be larger because they were used as garden plots. In 1903, when north Ballard was still relatively rural, the cow ordinance went into effect, prohibiting free-roaming cows south of Northwest Sixty-fifth Street; north of here, cows could still roam free. Currently, Ballard Avenue hosts the most popular year-round farmers' market in the state of Washington.

The coastline and beaches were, and still are, a major attraction of Ballard. Surrounded by water and maritime focused, Ballard favors boating and fishing. Ballard Beach, where Ray's Boathouse stands today, was a popular summer destination for day-trippers and campers. Golden Gardens beach was initially privately developed and promoted as a destination. In 1927, the City of Seattle Parks Department designated Golden Gardens a public beach.

There were no dedicated public parks in Ballard pre-annexation. Gilman Park was the first park designated by the City of Seattle. Due to clear-cutting of Ballard's forests for the shingle industry, Ballard had less public green space than any other district of Seattle and remained sparsely treed for decades. In the 1990s, the Re-Tree Ballard program provided many of the trees one sees in Ballard today. Groundswell NW, started by Lillian Riley, has worked to protect and increase open space in Ballard since its first "gray to green" project, which turned part of the parking lot behind the original Nordic Heritage Museum, located in the Webster School Building, into a playground in 1996. Sunset Hill Park exists thanks to a philanthropic donation of two blocks along the cliff; there, thousands of people enjoy the sunset view of the water and Olympic Mountains every year.

The City of Seattle purchased Golden Gardens Park from the Treat family in 1923 for the cost of $37,000. As a city park, Golden Gardens has seen many improvements. In 1929, a brick bathhouse, still there today, replaced a wooden one. By 1931, a long pergola paralleled the beach just west of the railroad tracks. In the late 1920s and early 1930s, the Sunset Gun Club even had a skeet shooting facility just north of the oil dock at the north end of the park. After the oil tanks, which were part of the railroad village Metum, were removed, the marshy land in the northern part of the park was filled in to provide the grassy meadow many enjoy today. Remnants of the oil refueling pier pilings are still visible. As seen in the above photograph, there was always swimming. At one point, there was even a Golden Gardens swim team. Today, those who partake in the annual polar bear plunge brave the chilly waters of Puget Sound on New Year's Day.

Everyone wants to be outdoors in Ballard's dry, sunny summertime weather. The popular Golden Gardens beach had easy access by streetcar. Visitors still use the Golden Gardens Bathhouse, shown in this 1920s photograph. Liberated from the long swimming skirts of previous years, these young women are wearing the figure-hugging, sleeveless woolen tank suits that idealized the androgynous athletic figure of 1920s fashion. Men, such as the one depicted here, also wore full tank suits made of wool jersey. The parasol behind the women was an exotic present from a seafaring relative. The Golden Gardens Bathhouse became a landmark in 2005.

Although Golden Gardens has changed considerably over the years and now has a breakwater, a marina, and port facilities, children still play at the water's edge just as these two did in 1923.

The Works Progress Administration (WPA) was a federally funded plan during the 1930s Great Depression and was designed by the Roosevelt administration to employee men and women who were out of work. Many beautifully constructed National Park buildings were constructed through this program. In Seattle, the WPA employed photographers to take pictures of every house and building in the city, identified by the address written across the image in white. This comprehensive pictorial record is available through the Puget Sound Archives. WPA funding also paid for half of the upgrade of the Ballard Bridge in the late 1930s. Additionally, WPA workers reinforced the sloughing cliff above Golden Gardens and built the stairs that go down to the beach from the end of Eighty-fifth Street NW, as shown in the photograph. (Courtesy of Seattle Municipal Archives.)

These women are inspecting the new waterfall built by the WPA on the cliff above Golden Gardens Beach. (Courtesy of Seattle Municipal Archives.)

The early days of Ballard saw many families migrating to the local beaches during the summer months. On the beach, they would build wooden platforms and erect tents on top. Some families would stay for a few days, and others stayed for weeks. Men returning to work would climb the hill to catch a streetcar or walk along the train tracks into town, while the women and children remained at camp sharing chores and recreation. On many a summer's evening, dances were held for the adults. This photograph was taken near the Hiram Chittenden Locks. The railroad bascule bridge seen in the background is still in use today.

These picnickers at Ballard Beach (the current location of Ray's Boathouse) are enjoying an outing in one of Seattle's chillier months. As they say in Norway, "There is no such thing as bad weather, only bad clothing!" When the locks were built in 1917, the railroad bridge was changed to the current-day bascule bridge, seen in the background of this photograph. The bridge opened to allow taller ships to enter and leave through the locks.

A trolley line (the Carbine) was extended to Loyal Avenue NW and Eighty-fifth Street NW to provide access to a path to the park at the north end of Shilshole Bay. Developed by Harry Treat, the park was meant as a destination, while a sales pitch was delivered on the way. An amusement park was located there at one time, near where families would camp. Later, for many years, a public bus ran down Shilshole Avenue to bring people to the beach. Sadly, there is no public transportation to Golden Gardens or Shilshole Marina today.

Ballard Beach was a popular retreat in the summer. Some families set up seasonal tents on the beach that functioned as summer homes. This is the current site of Ray's Boathouse restaurant.

Where once there was a ferry dock, Ray Lichtenberger moved his boat rental and bait house in 1939. He added a coffee house in 1945. By 1952, he had erected the iconic neon sign spelling out RAY'S in the bold-red letters that one sees today. The Ray's Boathouse sign has been the only constant as the original café evolved to fish and chips. Since those times, a nationally respected seafood restaurant emerged. The restaurant and upstairs café offer views of a pier at the entrance to the Ballard Locks and has been a popular spot for generations. In 1988, the restaurant suffered a four-alarm fire, which was witnessed for miles. Ray's rebuilt and even survived a smaller fire in 1997. (Courtesy of MOHAI.)

Early Ballard had more stumps than children. The 1890 US Census showed that children only accounted for 22 percent of Ballard's population. Young, single men working in the timber or fishing industries predominated. People over the age of 16 were recognized as adults since it was common for both males and females to leave home and become self-supporting at 15 or 16 years old.

Children could always find places to play in Ballard, either at the beach or in town. Children could catch frogs in the marsh next to the dairy near the locks, or they could play ball games in empty lots. Following adult fashion, children's fashion became much less cumbersome and inhibiting in the 1920s. Previously, as depicted in this turn-of-the-century photograph, boys wore knee-length trousers, called "longies," held up with braces, year-round, until they turned 16. Cold weather required knee-length, turned-over socks and woolen jerseys worn with the longies, while summer called for short-sleeved shirts and Fair Isle slipovers. Canvas shoes or sandals in the summer replaced Victorian lace-up boots.

These eight women posing in costume with bicycles around 1910 were probably part of a community play at the Ballard Field House. The Ballard Field House, forerunner to the Ballard Community Center next to Adams Elementary, offered classes, sports opportunities, and local theater.

Friends are out on a coastal hike around 1920. Hiking is still a favorite Ballard pastime.

As in many thriving communities in the early 1900s, Ballard residents liked to be outside playing games when they could. From a casual round of backyard croquet to baseball to Nordic skiing to hockey, the people of Ballard could not get enough of their sports. Ballard had its own hockey rink, and word of mouth was enough to entice players to play a game at the rink or on a frozen pond.

One can imagine these young women were imitating the popular band concerts held at Salmon Bay Park, one of two public parks in early Ballard. In those days, many family get-togethers and community and church socials with live music were held at a bandstand on a knoll beneath the tall trees.

BALLARD BAND BOX MILLINERY CO.

5408 22d Ave. N.W.   *Oldest and Most Up-to-Date Millinery Store in Ballard*

This postcard, postmarked October 4, 1909, was addressed to Mrs. T.H. Ryan at 6727 Thirteenth NW, Ballard. It is a promotional postcard with the following statement: "Dear Madam: Our stock is complete and up-to-date. Our designs are exclusive and correct. Our prices are moderate. We thank you for your former patronage and earnestly solicit your future orders. Respectfully, The BALLARD BAND BOX Designers of Exclusive Millinery."

This fashionably dressed mother was posing by a home, perhaps hers, located at Northwest Seventy-seventh Street and Fourteenth Avenue NW. While many homemakers knew how to sew and a number of women made a living as dressmakers and seamstresses, a selection of ready-made clothing was also available on Ballard Avenue. The Band Box Millinery offered women's hats, bonnets, scarves, gloves, and all of the other necessary accessories. It was common for both men and women to wear fur, and two local furriers operated in Ballard until the 1970s. Fur was popular in cold countries, and although the climate was milder here, Scandinavian fashion influenced a population with Scandinavian roots.

In 1921, the year of this photograph, a new law determined that one must be licensed to drive an automobile and drivers must be at least 16 years old. Drivers could obtain a license by submitting a form and paying $1. In the early days of the automobile, women often wore special driving attire; fashion recommended that a women's tweed or fur be coordinated with the interior of the car she was riding in. Men were often seen in "dusters," which were long overcoats that extended to the calves and were specifically designed to wear while driving. By the 1920s, cars had become much less of a novelty, and fashion was no longer specifically linked to the vehicle. This young woman is obviously dressed up and going places in this Ford Model T coupe!

After World War II, the widespread affordability of the automobile and highway construction precipitated a swift decline in public transit. Money and attention were redirected to roadways and away from other modes of transportation. This picture, taken during the Depression, depicts a 1918 Dodge and people picnicking in North Beach.

Ole Bardahl migrated to Ballard from Norway when he was just 20 years old. He worked first in the sawmills and then became a successful home builder. However, he was always interested in cars and improving their performance by reducing engine wear and increasing oil efficiency. He experimented and, in 1939, purchased a small chemical company in Ballard. By 1947, he had annual sales of $200,000. He used automobile racers to test his product and sponsored racing teams of all types. His hydroplane, named *Miss Bardahl*, won five gold cups and six national championships. The Bardahl Manufacturing sign has become iconic to Ballard. Driver Al Young has been sponsored by Bardahl Manufacturing Corporation for over 40 year as a drag racer and quasi-goodwill ambassador. Young believes that Ole Bardahl was "the most successful businessman in Seattle until Bill Gates." (Courtesy of Bardahl Oil.)

Similar to modern convenience stores, Ballard had many neighborhood grocery stores stocked with milk, bread, lard, eggs, and canned goods, and delivery service was standard. A horse-drawn carriage was a common form of transportation in the late 19th century. Horse-and-carriage delivery was followed by the bicycle and then quickly by the automobile. In 1900, the first automobile arrived in Seattle, and by 1904, automobile clubs started to replace bicycle clubs.

Located at the end of the streetcar line, H. Jacobsen Grocery at the corner of Thirty-sixth Avenue NW and Sixty-fourth NW Street was one of several food stores that were important to locals at the time.

In Ballard, there were numerous mom-and-pop grocery stores selling produce staples as well as small meat markets throughout the neighborhoods. Jones Brothers and Kastner's Meats were just two such local butcher shops where people shopped and could have meat delivered. Harold Nilsen grew up in Ballard, graduating from delivering the *Post-Intelligencer* to Safeway deliveries from his wagon when he was a child. After running a mom-and-pop at Seventy-fifth and Thirty-second Avenues, he and his family opened Nilsen's Foodliner at 6306 Thirty-second Avenue NW, billed as "Ballard's Most Modern Super Market." They were at the forefront of self-service, prepackaged meat, and a moving belt for speedy checkout. Kastner's Meats and Jones Brothers were local butchers who survived well into the 20th century.

The successes of Ballard's first lumber mill, Sinclair Mill; the Ainsworth's Seattle Steel and Iron Company; and the 1891 arrival of the railroad sparked a rapid population boom between 1890 and 1910. The influx of families created a growing demand for schools and materials for the classroom. The school board identified the parents of all children living outside the district and notified them that their children must pay advance tuition of $1.50 per month if they wished to attend Ballard schools. These funds developed several new schools over the next few years. In the days when many people did not attend beyond the eighth grade, this group of women, probably dressed in their finest for this 1900 high school graduation photograph, had a lot to be proud of.

Ballard High School dates back to 1901 when the Central School added upper grades. Home to the Ballard Beavers, it has been located at the northeast corner of Fifteenth and Northwest Sixty-fifth Streets since 1915 but was rebuilt in 1997, the same year the Ballard Foundation was funded to support educational programs, reunions, performing arts, and the finest art collection of any public high school. Their academies include maritime, biotech, finance, and engineering as well as a film/video program that is nationally known. From its victory gardens in World War II through its dedicated alumni, Ballard High School has kept over 120 years of community strongly connected. (Courtesy of MOHAI.)

Since its earliest years, Ballard High School has always boasted a strong dramatic presence. The rebuilt high school features the Earl Kelly Performing Arts Center, in honor of its beloved, longtime drama and humanities teacher from 1954 to 1987, Earl R. Kelly. Many award-winning artists credit their career to the inspiration and encouragement of their Ballard teachers, including Orre Nobles, another Northwest artist who taught at Ballard for 30 years and for whom the outstanding art collection is named.

This photograph depicts the 17th of May Parade on Ballard Avenue. The Syttende Mai celebration, or Norwegian Constitution Day, commemorates Norway's independence from Sweden and the signing of Norway's constitution at Eidsvoll on May 17, 1814. The triangular building featured in the center of the above image was once home to one of the region's moving companies, Ballard Livery and Transfer. Originally owned by B.J. Cooney and Son, the Boyd brothers took over in 1908. Their special was heavy hauling. With a staff of 20 employees and 10 horse-drawn carriages, they met the moving needs of Ballard and Seattle until 1918. Ballard Transfer was owned by several generations of Millers, moving everything from an elephant to entire houses; its last cargo was delivered in December 2019. An offshoot, Ballard Preferred Moving, still exists to move contents of the home, but not the home itself.

These women are marching in the 17th of May Parade on Ballard Avenue around 1905. They are dressed in Norwegian *bunads* (folk costumes).

Several children, each wearing a Norwegian folk costume, stand with a man dressed as a Viking. They are awaiting the start of the Syttende Mai Parade in 1977. Norwegian Americans in Ballard have been celebrating the holiday since before the community was annexed by the City of Seattle, with commemorations including a children's parade, speeches, and singing. Today, a 17th of May Committee, made up of community members, plans holiday-related events. Aside from Oslo, the Ballard celebration may be the largest Constitution Day event in the world. (Courtesy of the National Nordic Museum.)

The Ballard P-Patch Gnomes are marching in the 17th of May Parade to raise community awareness and funding needed to purchase the land farmed by community members for 40 years. Besides providing food for individual growers, this P-Patch donates 2,500 pounds of vegetables to the Ballard Food Bank and Ballard Senior Center annually. (Courtesy of Laura K. Cooper.)

The Ballard P-Patch (1976) was one of the first Seattle Community Garden Programs in a never developed space near where many produce gardens (and cows) flourished in earlier days. Our Redeemer's Lutheran Church, established in 1944, provided the land for the garden once it had acquired land at Eighty-fifth and Twenty-fourth Streets NW. The garden fit its mission of providing shelter after World War II and feeding the community, hence a long relationship that linked the P-Patch's 80 gardeners and Ballard Food Bank. In 2019, the P-Patch faced loss of its land due to the church's need for renovations to bring it up to code. Banded together as the Ballard P-Patches Gnomes, the gardeners organized to build community support and fundraise the $2 million needed to acquire the land. They did it, and along with Our Redeemer's Lutheran Church, they celebrated that "the beets would grow on." (Above, courtesy of Cindy Krugman; below, courtesy of Laura K. Cooper.)

The Bagdad Theatre at 2218 Market Street opened May 28, 1927, and remained in business until 1949. Along with the surrounding retail, it was credited with moving the commercial core from Ballard Avenue to Market Street. The theater showed movies and had 1,000 seats, a Wurlitzer organ, and Persian decor.

Originally built as the Majestic Theater in 1914, this business had the distinction of being the oldest continuously operating movie theater in the United States prior to its closure in 1997. As the Majestic, it had 1,000 seats, which were later reduced during its time as Bay Theater. Members of the Alhadeff family purchased the shuttered theater and erected a new Majestic Bay on the Market Street site, with the goal of restoring its glamour while providing an intimate, modern experience. The neon "Bay" letters from the longtime marquee were refurbished and incorporated into its outdoor signage. This photograph was taken during the pandemic of 2020. (Courtesy of Laura K. Cooper.)

Built in 1904 by notable architect Henderson Ryan, the Ballard Carnegie Free Public Library dominated the Ballard skyline for many years. With the help of a $15,000 grant from Andrew Carnegie and the dedication of the local Women's Christian Temperance Union, this library served this hardworking community until June 7, 1963. The building also functioned as a significant cultural and community center. Katherine Lund was a longtime librarian. After being under private ownership for decades, the building came up for sale in 2011. Ballard Historical Society teamed up with locally renowned architect Larry Johnson to prepare a landmark nomination. Over 40 letters in support of the nomination reached the Seattle Landmarks Preservation Board, thanks to outreach efforts by Historic Seattle, Ballard Historical Society, and the Washington Trust for Historic Preservation. The teamwork paid off and the Ballard Carnegie Library became a designated Seattle Landmark on November 7, 2012. Though it was too late to preserve the interior, the exterior of the building is landmarked and is no longer threatened by development or major change.

Booming communities need cemeteries, and they need hospitals. As with so many endeavors in Ballard, the acquisition of both were community driven. In the early years, doctors had private practices, usually in their homes. By 1928, the need was too great; community leaders sold stock to fund the first Ballard Accident and General Hospital, which would occupy space in the Eagles Building on Market Street. In the 1940s, board members acquired land on Tallman Street. In the 1950s, a Hospital Fund Drive Committee literally took to the street, with some 500 business and organization "Knuckle Knockers" soliciting pledges from neighbors every night and raising the money needed to build Ballard Community Hospital. Ballard Community Hospital merged with Swedish Medical Center in 1992. (Courtesy of MOHAI.)

By 1903, Ballard was already a bustling city of 10,000. Citizens formed the Crown Hill Cemetery Association and established a cemetery on a 10-acre knoll just north of Boundary Street (Northwest Eighty-fifth Street). The early acquisition has kept the "country in the city" with bountiful trees. (Courtesy of Laura K. Cooper.)

Florist Lillie Wiggins started Ballard Blossom in 1927 and operated the business until its sale to John Martin in 1947. Located first at Twentieth and Market Streets, the citywide florist moved to the former Middelstadt Mortuary at 1766 Northwest Market Street. The business is still family owned and now in just its third location on Northwest Eighty-fifth Street. (Courtesy of Ballard Blossom.)

Where once the default was Scandinavian goods throughout Ballard shops, there is now only one shop and café in Seattle dedicated to all things Scandinavian. Since 1962, Scandinavian Specialties has provided Nordic goods to the Pacific Northwest and beyond. This Fifteenth Avenue NW store offers a connection to the home countries of Scandinavia with its fresh meatballs, homemade fish cakes, brown cheese, authentic luncheon and coffee time foods, Swedish candy in bulk, and gifts. (Courtesy of Laura K. Cooper.)

Mike's Chili Parlor is a fourth-generation family business that started by serving the family chili recipe to shingle mill workers in the 1920s. Mike Semandiris arrived in Seattle in 1922 by way of Chicago after escaping from a Communist regime to Greece. In 1939, he was able to open Mike's Chili Parlor. There, he stuck to his simple menu (chili), which allowed the rest of his family to emigrate. This popular tavern provided the location for the Gene Hackman film *Twice in a Lifetime* and has been featured by the *Road Food* series. The *Road Food Guide* calls the urban chili parlor an endangered breed. (Above, courtesy of Seattle Municipal Archives.)

The Lockspot Café has the distinction of being one of the oldest continuously operating eateries not just in Ballard, but all of Seattle. It is housed in the 1886 residence of one of Ballard's earliest non-native families, the Bryggers (above), at the main gate to the Ballard Locks. Lockspot regulars span back generations. (Below, courtesy of Tod Gangler.)

Six

BYGONE BALLARD

Ballard has seen extraordinary growth and change in the last few decades. Thanks to a grant from King County's 4Culture Heritage Projects Program, the actual voices of many of bygone Ballard can be heard. In advance of Ballard's centennial, in 1988 a dedicated group of volunteers conducted oral histories of immigrants to Ballard. A portion of these oral histories were published in 2001 in *Voices of Ballard: Immigrant Stories from the Vanishing Generation*. Only 11 of the oral histories from 1988 had been excerpted.

Thirty-five years later, these recordings on tape cassettes were unearthed and digitized. Finding the source material (in the basement of the neighborhood center) yielded untold stories. In particular, recollections of early professional women and second-generation Ballard residents revealed a far more diverse population in terms of ethnicity and occupations. The King County grant allowed for these dusty cassette tapes to be digitized and made into electronic audio files. The final project will be an interactive map that allows users to listen to oral history with access to photographs, news clippings, and map locations pertaining to addresses mentioned in the narrative. The project will be an accessible archive through the Ballard Historical Society website.

So, what did the unexcerpted oral histories reveal? Interviewed in the home where she grew up and returned after her father's death, one woman recalled growing up in Polish Town during the Depression. Another previously untranscribed oral history brings to life a woman "born liberated," who, despite working in the Roosevelt administration, died without an obituary having outlived her siblings. In some cases, references within the oral histories led to research, which in turn revealed more discoveries and connections such as that between a lumber baron, a Japanese American who was incarcerated, and a Polish Town resident. This generation has vanished. However, thanks to the efforts of Ballard Historical Society, the interviews and stories of these bygone Ballardites are not lost.

The only clues to the woman's identity in this photograph from the Peterson Collection comes from a personal reminiscence by a Peterson—"That was Cula, before she went to Nome with her new husband." The Model T Ford offers another clue; it is from approximately 1920. This photograph also serves as a warning of how the past can be lost without documentation or proper preservation. The mission of Ballard Historical Society is to better preserve the past so people can discover its treasures in the present. No one wrote Cula's story, so she is an unknown part of bygone Ballard.

Brothers Eli T. and Joseph Alonzo Hamblet hailed from New York but became Ballard pioneers when they acquired land in 1840. Eli was a missionary in British Columbia where he met and married Mary, the daughter of a chief of the Kitsalas (one of the Tshumshian tribes). Mary was born in 1839 on Annette Island in Metlakatla, British Columbia. They were involved with the First Baptist Church in downtown Seattle while raising eight children and then grandchildren. Although some structures built for the family members remain, as well as streets Mary and Alonzo, much of their land became the site of Ballard High School and the town houses to the north. Rev. Eli Hamblet died the same year as his wife, as announced by a *Seattle Daily News* headline that seems odd for 1905: "Well Known Pioneer of Seattle and Early Ballard Dies Suddenly at Age of Eighty-Three Years." The nearby Ballard Baptist Church was their place of worship in their final years. This 1887 census reflects the year that all eight children were still at home. (Right, courtesy of Swedish Cultural Center; below, courtesy of United States Federal Census, National Archives and Records Administration 1887.)

Census of the Inhabitants in Salmon Bay, in the County of King, Territory of Washington.

Enumerated this 17th Day of May 1887.

By Geo. M. Bowen Dep. County Assessor.

	Names of persons residing in Washington Territory on the first Monday in April, 1887.	Age	M (Male)	F (Female)	White	Black	Mulatto	Citizen	Indian half breeds	Kanakas	Profession, Occupation or Trade, of Male or Female.	Married	Single	Nativity. State, Territory or Foreign Country.	Can not Read, age over 15 years.	Can not write, age over 15 years.	Deaf, Dumb, Blind, Insane or Idiotic.	Male citizens of US over 21 years of age.	Female citizens of US over 21 years of age.	Aliens over 21 years of age—Males.	Aliens over 21 years age—Females.
1	Grey, D. B.	22	/		/						Laborer	/		Canada						/	
2.	Goold John	33	/		/						Miner			Eng.						/	
3	Glackibn P.	56	/		/						Carpenter	/	/	Ireland						/	
4.	Hamblet, E. J.	66	/		/						Jahiner	/		N. Y.							
5	" Mary	46		/					/		Hswf	/		B. C.							
6	" Alonzo	24	/		/						Engineer		/	Wash. Ter.						/	
7	" E.	21		/					/		Seymstress	/		"							
8	" Joseph	20	/		/						Farmer		/	B. C.							
9	" A.	18		/					/		Seamstress		/	"							
10	" Jane	14		/					/					"							
11	" Dorcas	12		/					/					"							
12	" Eli	10	/		/									"							

"Father built his milk house over a stream." Born in 1896 Ballard to Icelandic immigrants Bogi and Hallfridur Bjornson, Margaret Wandrey witnessed cow fields and Ballard's boom. Her older sister Ellen, born in 1890, was the third registered birth in King County. From an early age, she took an interest in the stories of the area's pioneers, including her neighbor Eli Hamblet. She authored one of the few books on Ballard, *Four Bridges to Seattle: Old Ballard.* She wrote that many Ballard residents, including her father, kept dairy cows and took advantage of a stream to keep the milk cold. In this photograph, taken from the Magnolia side of Salmon Bay looking toward Ballard, dairy cows graze in the foreground of the engineering feat of the Government Locks. Cows ranged throughout Ballard until 1903, when the cow ordinance made it illegal for them to roam freely below Northwest Sixty-fifth Street.

The press always referred to Veida Morrow when covering her work as a trial attorney, City of Seattle lawyer, member of the Roosevelt administration, sportswoman, and developer. Her remarkable life was rediscovered when oral histories dating from 1988 were transcribed. This photograph is from the 1918 Ballard High School senior yearbook. Veida graduated at just age 16 and received her law degree from the University of Washington as a member of the class of 1924. She was often referred to as "Girl Attorney" in local press, including when defending her father and brother from assault charges in a bar fight. Veida Morrow was the attorney for Seattle and, later, special assistant to the attorney general in Franklin D. Roosevelt's administration. Back in Seattle, she was responsible for developing her father's Greenwood landholdings into shopping centers. She and her family founded the Northwest Wilderness Project in order to protect Goldmyer Hot Springs. Having outlived siblings and her husband, Veida Morrow Metcalf died in 1996 without an obituary at the age of 94 years.

Swedish immigrants O.G. and Hulda Peterson built
this 10-acre homestead in 1902 after purchasing
the land from Anna Brygger. Standing behind the
cornstalks are Hulda and her five children. O.G.
was a carpenter who worked building boats in
Ballard. One day, the owner asked for a volunteer
diver because his regular did not show up. O.G.
volunteered, even though he could not swim, and
spent the rest of his career hard hat diving in
the maritime industry from Alaska to California.
He and Hulda were active in the Ballard Baptist
Church. Their son Ted Peterson Sr., the boy
on the right of this 1908 photograph, worked
with his father as a diver and then became a
Washington state senator for the 45th District. He
ran as a dark horse candidate after being asked by
Ballardites who did not like their representative.
He won because he was well known for his love
of Ballard since he had knocked on so many
doors to gather money for various civic projects
over the years. After he retired, Ted Peterson
Sr. headed the community effort to bring the
Ballard's former city hall's bell back into place,
right where it used to be at the top of Ballard
Avenue by community fundraising the project.
This treasured icon of Ballard history now hangs
(and rings) proudly in Marvin's Garden Park.

The 1920 version of the *Shingle* yearbook featured a block print of trees. The school was housed in a new building as of 1916 but had already reached its capacity of 1,000 by the 1920s. What a boom, since its 1902 graduating class was just four students!

William R. Bolcom (1866–1944) was a lumber baron who lived large (known for cigars, drink, and Sousa marches). His mansion on Thirty-second Avenue NW had a wing large enough to entertain the Seattle Symphony; he was a great music lover. When the home burned in 1934, their grand piano, valued at $5,000 even back then, miraculously survived. His acquisition, the Canal Mill, had a tendency to burn, as well. He founded the Olympic Golf Club, entertained greatly, and lived his final days at the Ambassador Hotel. His story links closely with those of others in pre–World War II Ballard. William M. Bolcom's second wife was Ballard's Katherine Larsen. They had two sons, and a grandson is a Pulitzer-prizewinning composer. Katherine died a year before the fire that destroyed the mansion, located on the same grounds as their Mossyback Lodge. William's life intersects with that of Sakaye Matsuda (his gardener) and Mavis Shallow Tuck's father, Pete (his mill foreman). (Courtesy of MOHAI.)

The incarceration of Japanese Americans during World War II is a shameful chapter in West Coast history. Many citizens lost their homes and businesses due to incarceration. In the 1930s, a Japanese American community in North Seattle centered around Green Lake. By coincidence, there were two non-related Matsuda families who lived in Ballard and whose children attended Ballard High School. One family had greenhouses and a florist business on Fourteenth Avenue NW. The Sakaye (Frank) Matsuda family lived on Northwest Sixty-ninth Street and operated a dry-cleaning business on Thirty-second Avenue NW. Their three children attended Webster School and Ballard High. They were sent to Minidoka War Relocation Center in Idaho. Son Frank graduated in 1941 and was working for a mill at the time of Pearl Harbor. While at Minidoka, he joined the US Army and became part of the most decorated regiment in American history, the 442nd Regional Combat Team. Matsuda later received a Congressional Gold Medal. According to oral history, the neighbors on Sixty-ninth Avenue NW stored their belongings and watched after the home. The Matsudas were able to return to Ballard; their home still stands.

NELLIE M. MASON—Aud. Clean-up Squad 2, 3, 4; St. Car Comm. 4; Girls' Club Comm. 2, 3; Bank Rep. 1, 2, 3, 4; Big B 2, 3, 4; Attendance Clerk 3, 4. *Hobby*—Collecting salt and pepper shakers and dancing. *Ambition*—To travel the U. S. with D. E. S. ● CONNIE E. MATSON—Publicity Comm. 4; Roll Rep. 4; Sr. Glee 2, 3, 4; Fjord Frolics 2; Opera 2; Spr. Con. 3. *Hobby*—Trying to do my chemistry. *Ambition*—To grow a few more inches. ● FRANK MATSUDA— Class Rep. 4; Roll Room Pres. 3; Roll Rm. Sec. 2; Baseball 2; Intra. Basketball 2, 3; Foul Shooting 3. *Hobby*—Traveling, sports, and airplanes. *Ambition*—To own an airplane and travel.

Martin Nowicki was a blacksmith and immigrant from Poland. This home also served as his workshop—note the windmill. Nowicki was the first president of the Polish American Club of Seattle with original location in Ballard. An announcement about the founding of the Polish American Club in 1896 notes that Nowicki's instrumental band played for the occasion. This home was one of the few houses originally surrounding Salmon Bay Park, Ballard's only designated park in the 1890s. The two outbuildings, including the windmill, have been replaced by a double-car garage.

Maxine SHALLOW—"Skinny"—Stamp Rep. 3; Girl Reserves 1, 2, 3, 4. *Hobby*—Ice skating and skiing with Mary Ann. *Ambition*—To kill time in the nursery.

Frances SHANNON—"Sweetheart"—Roll Rep. 4; Serving Com. 2; Jr. Glee 3. *Hobby*—Palling around with Thelm. *Ambition*—To work for the F. B. I.

Ronald SHAW—"Ronnie"—*Hobby*—Photography. *Ambition*—To become a successful photographer.

In her 1988 oral history, Maxine Shallow Tuck detailed growing up in what was known as "Polish Town" in Ballard, the neighborhood southeast of Market Street (formally called Ross District). Already a second-generation Ballardite (her father, Pete Shallow, was born here in 1895), Maxine grew up at 367 Northwest Forty-eighth Street and had returned there until her death shortly after her interview. Her colorful stories included the neighborhood workarounds during Prohibition, raising chickens, Pearl Harbor and the Japanese American incarceration of fellow Ballard High School students, and her father's role as the manager of the Bolcom Mill.

Elihu and Vivian Spearman were considered Ballard pioneers. They built a home here in 1917 at a time when there were few black families. All of the Spearman offspring led groundbreaking lives. This photograph shows middle daughter, Izetta Spearman (Hatcher), on October 5, 1947, attending a jazz performance in an unidentified home. Izetta is third from left on the couch. (Floyd Standifer, standing, second from left, went on to become a giant on the Seattle jazz scene). The oldest sister, Florice Spearman, was one of the first two black women hired at Boeing. Izetta was a nurse and retired from Harborview. Austin graduated from the University of Washington School of Engineering. The youngest sister, Irene, was one of the first black graduates with a bachelor of science in medical technology. Izetta Spearman Hatcher's daughter Vicky returned from the family's US Army posting in Germany to complete her senior year (1962) at Ballard High. At left is Austin's signature across his Ballard high school yearbook photograph. (Above, courtesy of MOHAI.)

Chris and Vizi Complita are shown celebrating their 50th wedding anniversary at the family home on Sunset Hill in 1955. The Complitas emigrated from Dalmatia, now known as Dubrovnik, Croatia. Chris Sr. worked on construction of the Ballard Locks. Their first home was across from Ballard Beach, along the railroad tracks. Although rebuilt, the Sunset Hill family home is still in the Complita family. Louis and Mary Complita Sr. (far left) raised their family there, as did their son Louis Jr. The Complita family acquired a vintage photograph taken from offshore that includes a glimpse of the Tregoning Boat Company, a view of their first residence across from Ballard Beach, and the hillside address that would soon be their home and is today. Tregoning burned in 1926 and is now the site of the Ballard Elks. The Complitas have always been able to keep an eye on what is now called Shilshole Bay. (Both, courtesy of the Complita family.)

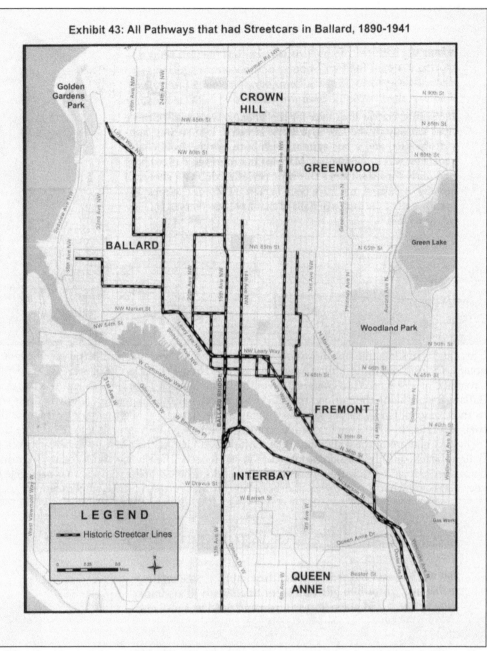

Exhibit 43: All Pathways that had Streetcars in Ballard, 1890-1941

For 50 years, from 1890 to 1941, Ballard had a streetcar system that connected it with downtown Seattle. The last streetcar ran along Eighth Avenue NW. The streetcars in west Ballard connected riders with Ballard Beach and its ferry as well as Ballard's train station and provided transport north to the Golden Gardens path. In addition, the streetcars connected downtown Ballard with Fremont, Crown Hill, and Greenwood. Although Ballard's population and density has greatly increased in the last 60 years, the subsequent transportation system has never kept pace. Seattle is finally building and expanding a light-rail system, but a Ballard line is not anticipated for another 20 years. (Courtesy of King County Metro.)

118

Private ferries traveled from the Ballard Beach area of Shilshole Bay to locations on the peninsula, for example to Suquamish (1928–1937) and Ludlow. Black Ball acquired the ferry line to Suquamish but then moved its terminus to Coleman Dock in downtown Seattle, and Ballard was outraged. The Ballard Commercial Club lobbied strongly for a ferry line. In addition to connecting Nordic communities, such as Poulsbo, the ferry facilitated dairy and produce imports from the Kitsap Peninsula and helped developers promote real estate on the peninsula. Ballard Beach ferries also prompted the extension of Market Street as a commercial route. (Courtesy of MOHAI.)

The hectic period of late-19th-century railroad construction ended with Seattle as the terminus of the Great Northern Railroad in 1893. The railroad opened the door to a record number of migrants flooding into Washington. Ballard used to have its own train stop on the railroad line that, since 1912, crossed the jackknife bridge south to the Magnolia side. An equipment shed is all that remains around the site of the station house. Until recently, one could still see the Ballard sign along the tracks while standing on the Fifty-seventh Avenue NW overpass. (Courtesy of MOHAI.)

The 1946 cover of Ballard High School yearbook, the *Shingle*, contrasted Ballard of the year 1916 (when the school was new) with Ballard 30 years later. The line drawing by Louise Molitor shows 1946 Market Street replete with automobiles of the time and a bus that had replaced the streetcars five years earlier.

The first Manning's Cafeteria opened in Seattle's Pike Place Market in 1908. At its peak, the chain stretched to 40 locations along the West Coast, including a location near Twenty-fourth Avenue NW and Northwest Market Street in the 1930s. Positioning itself for a more modern Ballard, in 1964 Manning's built a new cafeteria at the northwest corner of Fifteenth Avenue NW and Northwest Market Street. Referred to as Ballard's "Taj Mahal," Manning's architecture was known as Googie, and it was designed to attract attention. Googie referred to an architecture that originated in Southern California to embrace the future of the car and the jet. The location became a Denny's in 1984. An effort in 2008 failed to keep the building from demolition. A landmark status would have kept this surviving example of the flamboyant architecture. Despite its initial qualification by the Seattle Landmarks Preservation Board, the developers prevailed and an eight-story, mixed-use building occupies the corner. In its earlier Ballard location, a classified advertisement called for "waitresses, neat and attractive, ages 20–35." (Below, courtesy of Seattle Municipal Archives.)

The loss of the Manning's/Denny's building came at low point for Ballard as the owners of nearby Sunset Bowl had just announced the sale of its property to developers. Built in 1956, Sunset Bowl had already reached iconic status long before its proposed demise in 2008, having been featured in Pacific Northwest writer Tom Robbin's *Half Asleep in Frog Pajamas*. Following the sale and closure of Leilani Lanes in Greenwood, the loss of Sunset Bowl left North Seattle lane-less. During the heyday of bowling in Seattle, there were 30-some bowling alleys. As with the dance halls and skating rinks of early Ballard, once Sunset Bowl was gone there was no longer any sign that it had been a social center for decades. (Courtesy of Joe Mabel.)

The Viking Tavern at Sixty-fifth Street and Twenty-fourth Avenue joined the bygone list in 2013 after operating as a very local watering hole, also known for its food, since 1950. The tavern was typical of those still found on Ballard Avenue but that were formerly found throughout the neighborhood. Although the Viking was a single-story building, it was located close to many longtime apartments and was also known for where a neighbor could go to buy eggs. (Courtesy of Tod Gangler.)

Before the new National Nordic Museum was built at the foot of Twenty-eighth Avenue NW, a sprawling industrial building, commonly known as Fenpro, occupied this site. Originally a World War II munitions factory, over the years the factory produced aluminum products, including windows and road signs, and provided working-class jobs. During the 1990s, as industry began to shift out of Seattle, the wide and varied raw interior of the Fenpro warehouse hosted dozens of artists and fabricators, housing everything from small businesses to tiny painting studios. This unique and long-lasting community of creatives carried on in force until the building was demolished for the new museum in 2016. Denny Jensen, a metalworker, was one of the many artists/craftsmen who had a shop in the Fenpro Building. He was commissioned by Alaskan artist Steve Hendrickson to make metal flocks of geese and ducks that hang at the Juneau International Airport. (Above, courtesy of Abby Inpanbutr; below, courtesy of Peggy Sturdivant.)

Until 2021, Ballard had always had a newspaper that nearly every longtime Ballardite had delivered in the door-to-door days. The first news publications began in 1890, with the *News Echo* established in 1891. There were ownership and name changes. At one point, the *Ballard News* had its printing presses in the Cors & Wegener Building on Ballard Avenue. Meanwhile Mike Mitchell ran a later rival, the *Ballard Tribune*. The papers merged in 1963 to become *Ballard News Tribune*. The Robinson family purchased the paper in 1993 and managed to keep several local papers in print editions until 2021. In its online form, the *Westside Seattle* still provides the local news. (Courtesy of Robinson Newspapers.)

A woman holds three large king salmon at Sandy's Seafood market in Greenwood. Ballard women have always been willing to go the extra mile to get a good fresh salmon! There was the following saying: "If it's in the sea, you will find it in a freezer in Ballard." This photograph was taken around 1940.

In the mid-2000s, the story of an 83-year-old Ballard woman who rejected a million-dollar offer for her 1900 family home drew international attention. The home was a mere 1,550 square feet. Surrounded on three sides by the retail development called Ballard Blocks I, the home and woman at the center of the "Edith Macefield Story" prompted a documentary, music festival, book, art show, and tie-in to the Pixar movie *Up*. In truth, the woman with pancreatic cancer simply wanted to live out life at home, where her own mother had died. During this time, property owners who refuse to sell were called holdouts, and she became known as a local example. She willed the property to the construction manager whom she had come to rely on for errands. The house has changed hands several times since and gone through foreclosure. Macefield died in 2008; as of 2021, the house still stands but has never been reoccupied. Edith Macefield embodied the colorful history and independent spirit of Ballard. (Courtesy of Laura K. Cooper.)

ABOUT THE BALLARD HISTORICAL SOCIETY

The Ballard Historical Society, formed in 1988, is dedicated to preserving and celebrating the history of the Ballard community.

Ballard Historical Society has produced a walking tour brochure, created and maintained historic plaques on buildings in the landmarked district of Ballard Avenue, maintains a photograph archives, and hosts a classic home tour every three years. Other projects include Mapping Historic Ballard, a survey and online map of Ballard's 7,500 historic homes (homes at least 50 years old), and Mapping Ballard's Material Culture, an interactive overlay of oral histories and stories connected to some of the homes in the mapping survey.

There are many more longtime businesses and organizations in Ballard than are represented in this publication because the Images of America series is photograph-driven. It is Ballard Historical Society's greatest hope that this work will inspire others in preserving and sharing Ballard's past, and future, through valuable photographic records. To view more photographs like those featured in this book, to contribute to our historical photograph archives, or to become a member of the Ballard Historical Society, visit our web site at http://www.ballardhistory.org.

DISCOVER THOUSANDS OF LOCAL HISTORY BOOKS
FEATURING MILLIONS OF VINTAGE IMAGES

Arcadia Publishing, the leading local history publisher in the United States, is committed to making history accessible and meaningful through publishing books that celebrate and preserve the heritage of America's people and places.

Find more books like this at
www.arcadiapublishing.com

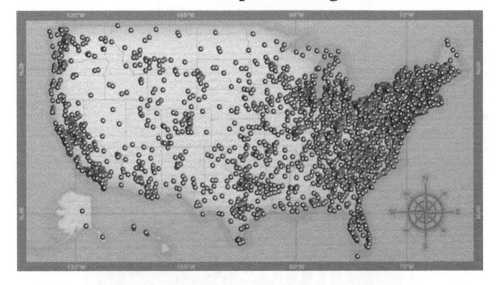

Search for your hometown history, your old stomping grounds, and even your favorite sports team.

Lightning Source UK Ltd.
Milton Keynes UK
UKHW020016220422
401880UK00003B/199